ENTREPRENEURS ANONYMOUS

ENTREPRENEURS ANONYMOUS

A Workaholic's Guide to
Building a Business That Runs Without You

KELLI LEWIS

Cover Designer: Pagatana Design Service

Book Interior and E-book Designer: Amit Dey—amitdey2528@gmail.com

Production & Publishing Consultant: AuthorPreneur Publishing Inc.—authorpreneurbooks.com

ISBN: 979-8-9935810-1-9 (Paperback)
ISBN:979-8-9935810-0-2 (eBook)
ISBN: 979-8-9935810-2-6 (Audio)

CONTENTS

INTRODUCTION

Picture this: A successful accounting firm owner helping clients manage their finances and grow their businesses while secretly drowning in her own financial chaos. Ironic, right? That was me, the expert behind KelliWorks, sitting in my office late one night, staring at yet another Uber Eats receipt: $1,100 in one month on takeout. Just one more sign that I had completely lost control of both my life and my money.

That receipt told a story far deeper than just food delivery. It was a mirror reflecting the state of my mental health, my loneliness, and the functional depression that had become my constant companion. You see, when we're not in a good mental space, our finances often become the first casualty. We spend mindlessly, seeking comfort in temporary fixes, something I've seen countless times in business owners' books. Meals and entertainment consistently show up as the largest, most frivolous category in small business spending. It's not just about the food; it's about what we're really hungry for.

There I was, finalizing a divorce, more overweight than I had been even after pregnancy, and navigating through Chapter 7 bankruptcy. Talk about rock bottom. The universe certainly has a sense of humor. I spent my days helping successful, wealthy, mindful entrepreneurs build their dreams while my own life was falling apart at the seams.

"KelliWorks, so you don't have to." Our tagline wasn't crafted in some fancy marketing meeting. Like everything authentic about our business, it came from genuine moments with clients. That's always been our way since 2009, when my first client watched me transform their manual booking process into an efficient, streamlined workflow and spontaneously exclaimed, "You work... your name should be KelliWorks!" My clients didn't just give me business; they gave me my identity.

And boy, did I work. Constantly. Clients were never the problem; they came steadily through referrals. I was their go-to person for everything: business and accounting, workers' comp audits, annual reports, past-due payroll issues, sales tax notices, you name it. My heart was in the right place (sounds super Zen and crunchy, I know), but I had become everyone's financial firefighter while my own house was burning down.

Here's the thing about being a natural problem solver: it's both a blessing and a curse. In my professional life, this gift opened doors, created opportunities, and built trust with clients. But personally? That's where things got complicated. I had to learn, sometimes the hard way, that not everyone wants to be fixed. This realization was part of the loneliness I felt. When you're always the one with solutions, it can create an invisible barrier between you and the people in your life. They see the problem solver, not the person who sometimes needs solving themselves. The irony wasn't lost on me. During quiet prayer time, I asked why I was surrounded by all these successful, high-vibrational people. Was it just to admire them? The answer hit me like a ton of bricks. I wasn't meant to admire them; I was meant to *become* them. Your gift will make room for you, as the saying goes, and mine had been preparing my path all along, even when I couldn't see it. That realization was my awakening.

I made the scariest decision of my life: investing money I didn't have in building the business I knew I could create. But this time, I approached it differently. No more cutting corners with part-time freelancers or well meaning friends and family members who "might be able to help." I learned that when you take your business seriously enough to invest in professional support, your team takes it seriously too.

Building a professional team isn't just about hiring people. It's about respecting your business enough to give it what it needs to thrive. When you pay for proper support, you're not just buying time or skills; you're investing in your company's future. I needed a real team that would show up as I showed up. (And let me tell you, the "gods of payroll" have never failed me, a little accounting humor for you there!)

Looking back now, I can see that I was on my road to success the whole time. Sure, I got out of the car sometimes, walked along the highway, did some sight-seeing, and played in the dirt. But the destination never changed. My gift was always meant to bring lightness into the lives of people surrounding their business and finances. Sometimes we need to trust that there's something bigger than ourselves rooting for us, paving the way. This isn't a religious or spiritual book, but I'll tell you this: believing in something greater than yourself can be the difference between staying stuck and soaring forward.

This book isn't just another business guide. It's a raw, honest roadmap from someone who has been in the trenches, from a 23-year-old who just wanted to help people to a small business expert who learned how to navigate the treacherous waters of entrepreneurship while maintaining faith, ethics, and character.

You'll learn how I transformed from the person who said "yes" to everything (while secretly struggling with it all) to someone who built systems, empowered teams, and created genuine work-life harmony. Because here's the truth: people do business with those they like, and your network is what will take you there.

In these pages, I'm sharing it all: the embarrassing mistakes, the late-night revelations, and most importantly, the practical strategies that helped me build a business that truly works. Whether you're drowning in operational chaos, feeling overwhelmed by your success, or still searching for it, this book is your permission slip to stop struggling and start thriving.

Ready to transform your business and life? Let's dive in. I promise to keep it real, make you laugh, and show you exactly how to build a business that works for your life, not against it. Thank you for being here. Thank you for choosing yourself.

CHAPTER 1

THE OWNERSHIP TRAP

"Click 'Receive Items' under the Purchasing menu, then select your open PO," I whispered, trying not to disturb my newborn son sleeping beside me. Less than 24 hours after bringing life into this world through a peaceful home birth, here I was, walking her through receiving a purchase order in QuickBooks Point of Sale instead of soaking in those precious first moments with my baby.

That wasn't dedication; that was desperation.

The dream of entrepreneurship often starts with a vision of freedom, being your own boss, making your own rules, and building something meaningful. Yet somehow, that dream morphs into a reality where you're more trapped than ever before. Welcome to what I call the ownership trap.

The Reality of Entrepreneurial Burnout

The thing about the ownership trap is that it feels deceptively like success. After all, isn't being busy a sign that business is good? Talk to any seasoned entrepreneur, and they'll tell you it's actually the number one myth that keeps business owners stuck: this belief that working harder equals working better.

I was pumping milk while driving between client appointments. That's not dedication; that's desperation. Ask any business owner who's made it to the other side, and they'll share similar stories of those early days. We all think these sacrifices are the price of success. But here's the truth: It's actually the price of not having proper systems in place.

You know what I'm talking about. Those endless nights answering emails, the weekends spent catching up on paperwork, the vacations where your laptop becomes your closest companion... We wear these badges of exhaustion like honors, proudly telling anyone who will listen how we "hustled" our way through another week. But let's call it what it really is: a slow-burning crisis.

Why Working Harder Isn't the Answer

Here's the painful truth I learned the hard way: You can't outwork a broken system. Think about it. When your car breaks down, do you get out and push it harder? Of course not. Yet that's exactly what we do in our businesses. We push harder, work longer, and sacrifice more, thinking that if we just give it that extra push, everything will fall into place.

I see it all the time, entrepreneurs who believe their business would collapse without their constant attention. They're the first ones in and the last ones out. They handle everything from high-level strategy to ordering office supplies. And yes, their businesses often survive, sometimes even thrive in terms of revenue. But at what cost?

The real irony? This all-consuming approach actually limits your business's potential. When you're buried in day-to-day operations, you can't see the opportunities for growth, innovation, or efficiency that are right in front of you. It's like trying to map out a city while crawling on your hands and knees, you're too close to see the big picture.

The solution isn't to work harder or longer. It's not about finding that magical productivity hack or time management app. The real answer lies in fundamentally changing how you view your role as a business owner. It's about building a business that can thrive without your constant presence, not one that depends on your perpetual sacrifice.

Think of it this way. Your business should be like a well-oiled machine where you're the engineer, not the engine. Your job isn't to power everything through sheer force of will. It's to design, maintain, and improve the systems that keep things running smoothly.

The first step? Acknowledging that being trapped isn't a rite of passage. It's a sign that something needs to change.

From Survival Mode to Strategic Thinking

Here's the stark difference between working IN your business versus working ON it: When you're in survival mode, you're the firefighter, the technician, and the go-to person for every little thing. Most business owners get stuck here, spending their days putting out fires instead of preventing them. And guess what? The more time you spend on daily operations, the less your business grows. When you're thinking strategically, you're the architect, designing systems that prevent fires in the first place.

The truth? My clients didn't need me to sacrifice my postpartum recovery or pump milk between appointments. They needed systems and strategies that would give them clarity. Ironically, they're happier now with those systems than they ever were with my 24/7 availability.

This shift from survival to strategy isn't just about working differently; it's about thinking differently. When you're caught in the daily grind, your horizon shrinks to the next hour, the next day, or maybe the next week if you're lucky. Strategic thinking requires you to lift your head up and look months, even years, ahead. It's the difference between frantically answering client emails at midnight and creating an automated onboarding system that anticipates and answers their questions before they even ask.

Understanding the Difference: Working IN vs. Working ON Your Business

When you're working IN your business, you're:

- Responding to every client email personally.
- Handling day-to-day operations manually.
- Making all decisions, big and small.
- Being the bottleneck for every process.

When you're working ON your business, you're:

- Creating systems that handle routine tasks.
- Building teams that can operate without you.
- Developing strategies for growth.
- Leading rather than doing.

Talk to any thriving business owner, and they'll tell you the same thing: everything changed when they stepped back and started working *on* their business instead of *in* it. The transformation isn't just about revenue; it's about reclaiming your life.

As Michael Gerber, author of the iconic book *The E-Myth Revisited*, powerfully articulates, "The fatal assumption is that an individual who understands the technical work of a business can successfully run a business that does that technical work." This profound insight cuts to the heart of why many entrepreneurs find themselves trapped in day-to-day operations, unable to see the bigger picture.

The Emerging Role of AI in Business Transformation

While not explicitly part of this narrative, it's worth noting that we are standing at the precipice of a technological revolution. Artificial intelligence is quietly reshaping how businesses operate, offering unprecedented opportunities for entrepreneurs to work smarter, not harder. The most successful business leaders of tomorrow will be those who learn to harness these technologies, using them as a strategic lever to create more value with less direct intervention.

Common Pitfalls That Keep Business Owners Stuck

One of the biggest traps I fell into was carrying over the employee mindset into my role as CEO. When I worked for others, giving my all was expected and praised. But here's the hard truth I learned, from one CEO to another: my clients didn't respect me as their equal because I didn't respect myself. My prices were too low, and I was giving everything away in the name of dedication.

I've noticed, time and time again, that almost every new business owner starts by undercharging and overdelivering. They loved me, sure, but love without respect is merely appreciation. And appreciation doesn't build sustainable businesses.

The real trap lies in those seemingly innocent habits we carry over from our previous roles: the need to be constantly available, the compulsion to do everything ourselves, and the belief that working longer hours equals better results. These aren't just bad habits; they're business killers in disguise.

Take the "superhero syndrome," you know, being available 24/7 and responding to every client message within minutes. I used to think this made me indispensable. Instead, it made me a commodity. Or consider the "discount dance," saying yes to lower rates because you're afraid of losing business. Each discount becomes a precedent that's harder and harder to break.

Then there's the perfectionism trap. You spend hours tweaking that proposal or refining that process, convinced that if it's not perfect, it's not good enough. Meanwhile, opportunities slip by, and your business remains stuck in place. Perfect isn't just the enemy of good; it's the enemy of growth.

But here's the thing: These pitfalls aren't character flaws; they're growth opportunities. They're the growing pains of transitioning from employee to entrepreneur, from technician to CEO. The path forward starts with a simple but powerful shift, seeing yourself not as a service provider but as a business owner. Not as someone who works for their clients, but as someone who partners with them.

Signs You're Stuck in the Trap

Over-Involvement in Day-to-Day Operations

You might be stuck in the ownership trap if:

- Your phone is the first thing you check in the morning and the last thing you see at night.
- You can't remember the last time you took a vacation without your laptop.
- Your family has stopped asking if you'll make it to dinner.
- You're so involved in every detail of your business that you can't step away for a day.
- Your team waits for your approval on even the smallest decisions.

Let's be honest, these aren't badges of honor; they're warning signs, like the check engine light on your car that you've been ignoring for months. The most dangerous part? This level of involvement can feel necessary, even virtuous. After all, isn't it good to be deeply invested in your business?

But here's what's really happening: You've become the bottleneck in your own company. When every email needs your attention, every decision requires your approval, and every client demands your personal attention, you haven't built a business; you've built a job. And it's probably the most demanding job you've ever had.

Feeling Irreplaceable: The Fear of Delegation

The most telling sign isn't just being busy; it's the anxiety that creeps in when you try to step away. You know that pit in your stomach when you think about taking a real vacation? That's not dedication; that's dependency. Your business has become dependent on you, and you've become dependent on being needed.

I see this pattern repeat itself with almost every entrepreneur I work with. They've mastered their craft so well that they can't imagine anyone else doing it "right." Every task becomes a non-delegable priority because "it's just faster if I do it myself." Sound familiar?

The real kicker? This mindset is self-reinforcing. The more you do yourself, the less your team develops the confidence and competence to take things off your plate. They become trained to wait for your input, creating a cycle where you're increasingly essential to every aspect of the business.

Think about it. When was the last time you:

- Spent an entire day working on business strategy rather than in operations?
- Took a complete weekend off without checking in?

- Let your team handle a major client situation without your involvement?
- Made it through dinner without checking your phone?

If these questions make you uncomfortable, you're not alone. But discomfort is often the first sign that something needs to change. Being irreplaceable isn't a strength; it's a liability, both for your business and for your well-being.

The truth is, a business that can't run without you isn't sustainable. It's not scalable. And most importantly, it's not giving you the freedom you probably dreamed about when you started this journey. The good news? Recognizing these signs is the first step toward breaking free. And believe me, there is a way out, but it starts with acknowledging where you're stuck.

The Cost of Staying Trapped

How Burnout Impacts Your Business, Health, and Relationships

Let me be brutally honest: I was going through bankruptcy while helping other businesses thrive. The irony wasn't lost on me. I was resentful, exhausted, and broke. Not exactly the entrepreneurial dream, right? What I've learned, and what so many other business owners discover too late, is that working longer hours often leads to diminishing returns, both financially and personally.

Imagine sitting at your son's graduation, phone in hand, answering client calls. That was me. I was everywhere and nowhere at the same time. When you're trapped in your business, you're:

- missing life's important moments
- constantly anxious about work
- physically present but mentally absent
- running on empty while pretending to be full.

The cost isn't just emotional; it's physical too. Those stress headaches become migraines. The occasional insomnia becomes chronic sleep deprivation. That tight shoulder becomes full-blown burnout. And let's talk about the relationships that suffer, marriages strained to the breaking point, children who stop trying to get your attention, and friendships that slowly fade away because you've missed one too many catch-ups.

But here's the real gut punch: All this sacrifice often leads to mediocre business results. You're working yourself to death just to maintain the status quo. It's like running on a treadmill; lots of effort, but you're not actually going anywhere.

The Hidden Opportunity Costs of Micromanagement

I was so busy doing the work that I couldn't see the opportunities right in front of me. Every successful business owner I know has had this same revelation, when you're caught up in the daily grind, you're missing countless chances for growth that are right in front of you.

Think about what you're really losing when you're stuck in the weeds of your business. That potential partnership you were too busy to explore? Someone else seized it. That market trend you noticed but were too overwhelmed to act on? Your competitor built their growth strategy around it. That innovative idea your team member suggested? It died in your inbox because you were too caught up in daily operations to give it proper attention.

The most expensive price tag of micromanagement isn't the time you waste; it's the growth you prevent. When you're controlling every detail, you're not just limiting your own potential. You're capping your entire organization's ability to innovate, adapt, and evolve.

Remember those team members waiting for your approval on every decision? They're not just wasting time; they're losing the confidence and capability to think independently. Your business isn't just missing opportunities; it's actively training your people to be dependent rather than innovative.

Every hour spent on tasks someone else could do is an hour not spent on what only you can do: setting vision, building relationships, spotting opportunities, and steering your business toward growth. When you're trapped in the day-to-day, you're not just tired; you're expensive. Your time, energy, and attention are being spent on $20-per-hour tasks while $2,000-per-hour opportunities slip away unnoticed.

The bitter truth? The cost of staying trapped isn't just about what you're doing. It's about what you're not doing. It's about the strategic thinking that never happens, the innovations that never materialize, and the growth that remains just out of reach. It's about building a business that's surviving when it could be thriving.

The good news? Once you recognize these costs, you can start making different choices. But first, you have to be willing to face the truth: the price of staying trapped is far higher than the cost of breaking free.

The Mindset Shift

The game changer came when I introduced tiered pricing packages. Want to know something shocking? Clients consistently chose the more expensive packages. Why? Because they valued clear, structured service more than my 24/7 availability. The structure is attractive. Boundaries are attractive. Professional systems are attractive.

This revelation challenged everything I thought I knew about client service. All those late-night emails I had been proud of? It turns out they weren't just unnecessary; they were actually undermining my value proposition. Clients don't want a frazzled business owner. They want a confident leader with clear processes.

Embracing the Idea That Your Business Can Run Without You

My first real step toward freedom was building an in-office team. While many in our industry went virtual (which works great for some), I knew I needed my team to physically see how "KelliWorks, so you don't have to." This wasn't just about hiring help; it was about creating a sustainable system.

The hardest part wasn't finding the right people. It was trusting them to maintain my standards. Every time I stepped back, my inner control freak would scream, "But they won't do it exactly like you!" And you know what? They didn't. Sometimes they did it better. That was a humbling lesson in itself. My way wasn't always the best way.

The Power of Letting Go and Building for Sustainability

When I started setting boundaries, some clients left. But remember those "payroll gods"

I mentioned? They never failed me. As the old clients phased out, new ones arrived. Clients who:

- Expected to work with a team, not just with me.
- Respected boundaries.
- Responded promptly to maintain service quality.
- Paid higher rates for better-structured services.

What I've seen, and what other business owners confirm, is that when you build the right systems and set proper boundaries, both client satisfaction and retention actually improve. It seems counterintuitive, but it's true. This shift isn't just about working less; it's about working smarter. When you build systems that can run without you, your business becomes more valuable, not less. Think about it. Which business would you rather buy, one that falls apart the moment the owner takes a vacation, or one with documented processes and a trained team?

The real mindset shift occurs when you stop seeing yourself as indispensable and start viewing yourself as a visionary. Your job isn't to be the best at doing the work. Your job is to be the best at building a business that performs the work excellently, consistently, and profitably.

Here's what nobody tells you about letting go: It's not a single decision; it's a daily practice. Every morning, you'll face choices that either pull you back into the weeds or push you toward true ownership. Choose wisely because the difference between a business that owns you and a business that serves you isn't in the hours you work. It's in the systems you build and the boundaries you maintain.

Remember: Your clients are not paying for your sacrifice. They're paying for your expertise, delivered through efficient, professional systems. When you embrace this truth, you're not just changing your business model; you're changing your life.

Your First Steps to Freedom

Ready for some tough love? You need to identify what is really holding you back. For me, it was the fear of losing control and the addiction to being needed. But here is what I discovered: When you provide clear, structured service packages, implement proper systems, and trust your team, your business actually works better without your constant involvement.

Implementation Timeline

Week 1–2

- Audit your current time usage
- Identify tasks that can be delegated
- Document your most common processes

Week 3–4

- Create service packages and pricing tiers
- Begin team training on key processes
- Implement basic systems and tools

Week 5–6

- Communicate changes to existing clients
- Start delegating routine tasks
- Establish regular team meetings

Week 7–8

- Review and adjust systems as needed
- Focus on strategic planning
- Celebrate small wins and progress

Remember: If you're answering client calls during life's big moments (like I did at my son's graduation) or handling work tasks when you should be recovering (like I did the day after giving birth), you're not dedicated; you're trapped. The good news? The way out starts with recognizing where you are.

Your business should support your life, not consume it. When I finally learned this lesson, I built a better business and a better life. And trust me, your clients will respect you more for it.

Take Action Now:

1. Identify three tasks you can delegate this week.
2. Set specific work hours and communicate them.
3. Create one system to handle routine requests.
4. Schedule dedicated time for strategic planning.
5. Start documenting your most common processes.

Your freedom journey starts now. What is the first thing you're going to change?

CHAPTER 2

THE KELLIWORKS PHILOSOPHY

In the business world, trust travels fast. When an entrepreneur finds someone who delivers real value and truly has their back, word spreads like wildfire. That's how KelliWorks grew from a single client's trust into what it is today. Not from a grand business plan or dreams of entrepreneurship, but from something far more powerful: the simple act of being trustworthy.

I never set out to build a business empire. In 2009, when the recession hit and my workplace crumbled, I simply did what my mother had always taught me: focus on your reputation and treat others the way you'd want to be treated. Little did I know that this fundamental principle would become the cornerstone of what we now call the KelliWorks Way.

My mother's wisdom about reputation has guided every decision I've made. In nearly two decades of serving clients, I can count on one hand the number who have left on unfavorable terms. And even those? They would still pick up my call today. That's not by accident; it's by design, a design built on character, not just competence.

There's an interesting paradox in accounting. While we work with numbers all day, our greatest successes have come from focusing on the human side of business. Although our industry tends to concentrate on spreadsheets and bottom lines, I learned early on that business is fundamentally about people. The relationships we've built and the trust we've earned, these aren't things you can quantify on a balance sheet, but they are the true measures of success. When you genuinely care about people's success, everything else tends to fall into place. Don't take my word for it; our clients express it best in their reviews, sharing stories of how this approach has impacted their businesses and lives.

But here's something that might surprise you: My secret to client satisfaction isn't just about how we treat clients; it's about how we treat our team. I always put my team first, even when finances are tight. Some might see this as inefficient, but I've learned that taking care of your team means they will take exceptional care of your clients. It's a simple formula, really, valued team members create valued client experiences.

Building Your Foundation: The Heart of Business Ownership

Before we explore the KelliWorks Way, let's talk about what matters most: your foundation as a business owner. This isn't just another business exercise; it's a moment to reconnect with why you started this journey in the first place.

Take a moment, breathe, and consider:

Service and Purpose

I remember sitting in my first office, really just a desk in the corner of my tiny bedroom, asking myself these same questions. They changed everything about how I approached business:

1. If money weren't a factor, what part of your business would you still do for free? This isn't just about passion; it's about identifying your core value proposition. For me, it was watching the relief on clients' faces when they finally saw me handle something they had been struggling with or a daunting task they hadn't been able to manage. What's that moment for you?
2. What drives you to keep going when things get tough? This is your anchor in stormy seas. When cash flow is tight, when clients are demanding, and

when everything seems overwhelming, what keeps you moving forward?

3. How has your purpose evolved since you first started? Your initial "why" might have been survival or independence, but now? Maybe it's about creating opportunities for others or changing your industry for the better.

Character and Values

These questions cut to the heart of who you are as a business owner:

1. What promise would you never break, even if breaking it meant more profit? This is your non-negotiable, your line in the sand, and the principle that defines not just what you do, but how you do it.
2. How do your current business practices reflect your personal values? Look closely here. Sometimes we inherit industry practices that don't align with who we really are. Now is the time to spot those disconnects.
3. What would your closest clients say about you when you're not in the room? This isn't about reputation management; it's about legacy building. The whispered conversations tell the real story of your business's impact.

Legacy and Impact

Think bigger than quarterly profits:

1. Twenty years from now, what do you want people to remember about your business? This isn't just about memory; it's about meaning. What mark do you want to leave on your industry, your community, and your world?
2. How are you contributing to your industry beyond making a profit? Perhaps you're mentoring newcomers, raising standards, or introducing innovative practices. Your influence extends beyond your client list.
3. What business practice do you follow that might seem "inefficient" but aligns with your values? Sometimes, the most meaningful aspects of our business don't show up on the bottom line. At least, not immediately. What do you do simply because it's right?

Your answers to these questions matter more than you might think. They're not just reflections; they're the building blocks of a business that works for you, not against you. As we move forward, let them guide you in creating something truly extraordinary.

Think of these questions as your business compass. When you're clear on your direction, decisions become easier, and priorities align naturally. The path forward, while not always easy, becomes clearer.

I've seen countless business owners transform their operations after deeply considering these questions. One client realized that her endless availability was actually contradicting her value of family time. Another discovered that his "inefficient" practice of personally checking in with every new client was, in fact, his biggest differentiator in the market.

These aren't just philosophical musings; they're practical foundations. Every system we build, every process we create, and every boundary we set should reflect these core truths about who you are and what matters most to you.

Take time with these questions. Write down your answers and share them with your team. Let them guide your decisions moving forward. When your business aligns with your deepest values and highest aspirations, that's when true success begins to flow.

The "KelliWorks" Philosophy

What It Means to Work Smarter, Not Harder

"Work smarter, not harder" might sound like a cliché, but let me share a simple story that illustrates exactly what this means in practice.

One of our clients had an employee spending 8 to 10 hours every week on payroll processing. That's essentially a full workday lost to administrative tasks. The employee was working harder, staying late, and double-checking figures, doing everything "right" by traditional standards. But here's what working smarter looked like. We implemented a time-tracking system and created a simple PDF-to-Excel conversion process. The result? The same task now takes just 1.5 hours per week. That's not just saving time; it's liberating potential.

One of the biggest misconceptions I see entrepreneurs struggle with is the belief that sacrifice equals success. There's a persistent myth that working longer hours, missing family dinners, and burning the midnight oil somehow translates directly to wealth. As Nathan W. Morris wisely noted, "It's not always that we need to do more, but rather that we need to focus on less."

At KelliWorks, working smarter means:

- **Automating Repetitive Tasks:** We transformed our client onboarding process from a manual task that took days into an automated workflow. New clients now receive welcome packets, scheduling links, and resource access automatically. No more endless email chains.
- **Creating Systems That Scale:** Instead of handling each client's books differently, we developed standardized processes that work across industries.

This means our team can support more clients without sacrificing quality or burning out.

- **Focusing on High-Impact Activities:** We identified which activities actually move the needle. For example, spending an hour reviewing strategic opportunities with a client creates more value than spending that same hour reconciling transactions (which we have now automated).
- **Eliminating Unnecessary Steps:** Remember those monthly reports that took hours to compile? We discovered that clients really only needed three key metrics. Now, we have dashboards that display these metrics in real time.
- **Building Processes That Can Be Delegated:** Every process we create follows a simple rule: If someone else can't understand it in five minutes, it's too complicated. This approach has allowed us to grow without becoming bottlenecked.

But here's the thing about working smarter: It requires you to question everything you've been taught about running a business. And that brings us to an uncomfortable truth. Many traditional business models are actually designed to keep you working harder, not smarter. Let's discuss why that is, and more importantly, what you can do about it.

Building a Business That Works Without You

Remember that payroll example we discussed earlier? That's just the tip of the iceberg. Building a business that operates independently of you isn't about finding a few clever shortcuts. It's about fundamentally rethinking how your business functions. Let me show you what this looks like in practice.

The Role of Systems in Business Freedom

When I first started implementing systems, I made every mistake in the book. I tried to automate everything at once, overwhelmed my team with complex procedures, and created documentation that was so detailed it was practically unreadable. However, through trial and error, we developed something that actually works.

The Freedom Framework

First, your business should be a system of systems. At KelliWorks, we've developed what I call the Freedom Framework:

1. **Document Everything:** Every process, decision, and workflow needs to be documented so clearly that anyone could follow it. Think of it as creating an operator's manual for your business. We don't just write procedures; we create visual guides,

video tutorials, and step-by-step checklists that make training and delegation seamless.

2. **Automate the Predictable:** If a task is repeated more than twice, we ask: "Can this be automated?" For example:
    - Client onboarding sequences
    - Regular report generation
    - Follow-up communications
    - Data entry and reconciliation
    - Schedule management
3. **Delegate the Rest:** What can't be automated should be delegated. But delegation without documentation is delegation to disaster. We create clear responsibility matrices and decision-making frameworks that empower our team to handle 85% of situations without needing my input.
4. **Monitor, Don't Manage:** Set up dashboards and reporting systems that give you visibility without requiring your involvement. This means:
    - Real-time performance metrics
    - Automated quality checks
    - Client satisfaction tracking
    - Team productivity measures

Creating Processes for Efficiency and Scalability

Let me share a real example of how this works. When we were smaller, I personally handled all client communications. Every email, every update, and every check-in call came from me. Does that sound familiar? However, as we grew, this became unsustainable. Here's how we transformed this using the Freedom Framework:

1. **Documentation Phase**
   - We analyzed my email patterns and identified common client scenarios.
   - Created templates for 80% of routine communications.
   - Developed decision trees for handling client concerns.
   - Built a knowledge base of FAQs and solutions.
2. **Automation Phase**
   - Implemented automated welcome sequences.
   - Set up scheduled check-in emails.
   - Created triggered alerts for important client milestones.
   - Built automated reporting schedules.
3. **Delegation Phase**
   - Trained team members on client communication standards.

   - Created clear escalation protocols.
   - Established team leads for different client segments.
   - Implemented regular team training sessions.
4. **Monitoring Systems**
   - Set up client satisfaction surveys.
   - Created response time tracking.
   - Implemented quality review processes.
   - Established weekly performance metrics.

The Result? True Freedom

When these systems work together, something magical happens. Youyou shift from being the person who does the work to the person who improves the work. Your role becomes strategic rather than tactical.

Here's what this looked like for me. Last summer, I took a three-week vacation, my first real break in years. Not only did the business continue to run smoothly, but our client satisfaction scores actually improved. Why? Because the systems we built were more reliable than any individual could be.

Remember: The goal isn't to remove yourself completely; it's to choose when and how you engage with your business. You want to work in your business because you want to, not because you have to.

Think about it this way. Every hour you spend building these systems is like making a deposit in your freedom bank. Initially, it feels like more work. You're not just doing the task; you're documenting it, creating processes, and training others. But over time, these deposits compound. Suddenly, you're not just saving hours; you're creating possibilities.

The transformation doesn't happen overnight. Start with one process, one system, and one delegation at a time. Focus on progress, not perfection. Because here's the truth: a good system, consistently executed, beats a perfect system that exists only in your head.

Your business should be like a well-conducted orchestra. It doesn't need the conductor to play every instrument, but it does need someone to ensure that all the parts work harmoniously together. That's your real role as a business owner.

The Power of Collaboration

Let me share something that changed everything for KelliWorks: I stopped trying to be the hero of every story and started being the guide for my team's success stories instead.

From Command to Collaboration

Traditional business models love their organizational charts, those neat little pyramids with the owner perched at the top. But here's what I discovered: The most powerful position isn't at the top of the pyramid; it's at the center of the circle.

When I shifted from giving orders to fostering collaboration, something remarkable happened. Team members who used to ask, "What should I do?" started saying, "Here's what I think we should do." That's not just a change in language; it's a transformation in ownership.

The Trust Dividend

Here's a truth that took me years to learn: Trust isn't just given or earned; it's invested. Every time you:

- ask for input instead of giving instructions
- allow team members to solve problems their way
- share the "why" behind decisions
- celebrate innovative thinking (even when it fails)

...you're investing in what I call the Trust Dividend. And like any good investment, it compounds over time.

Creating Ownership Mindset

At KelliWorks, we transformed our approach through:

- **The Solutions Circle:** Instead of having me solve every problem, we created weekly solution circles where team members present challenges and collectively develop solutions. The rule is simple: the person closest to the problem often has the best solution.

- **Skill Sharing Sessions:** Every team member becomes both a teacher and a student. Our bookkeepers teach our client service team about financial basics, while our client service team teaches the bookkeepers about communication strategies. This cross-pollination of skills creates a more versatile and understanding team.
- **Decision-Making Frameworks:** We developed clear frameworks that empower team members to make decisions independently. Instead of asking for permission, they use these guidelines to make confident choices that align with our values.

The Results Speak for Themselves

When you truly embrace collaboration:

- Innovation comes from everywhere, not just the top.
- Problems get solved faster because solutions don't have to flow through a single channel.
- Team members stay longer because they feel valued and heard.
- Clients receive better service because they're supported by an engaged team, not just one person.

Letting Go of Control

Let me tell you about my biggest business mistake, one that cost me years of growth and countless nights of sleep. I thought being a great business owner meant having my hands in everything. Spoiler alert: it doesn't.

The Control Paradox

Here's the truth that every successful entrepreneur eventually faces: the tighter you hold onto control, the less control you actually have. It's like trying to hold water in your fist; the harder you squeeze, the more it slips through your fingers.

When I started KelliWorks, I checked every spreadsheet, reviewed every email, and personally handled every client concern. I thought I was maintaining quality. In reality, I was becoming the biggest bottleneck in my own business.

The Fear Factor

Let's be honest about what really keeps us hanging on:

- Fear of mistakes
- Fear of losing client relationships
- Fear of things being done differently
- Fear of becoming replaceable

But here's what I learned: these fears cost more than the occasional mistake ever could. They cost you:

- Growth opportunities
- Team development
- Personal freedom
- Innovation potential

Breaking Free: The Trust-Building Blueprint

At KelliWorks, we developed a systematic approach to letting go:

- Start Small, Scale Smart: Begin with low-risk tasks and gradually increase responsibility. We use what I call the "Watch One, Do One, Teach One" method:
    - Team member observes the process
    - Performs it under supervision
    - Teaches it to someone else
- Clear Communication Frameworks: Establish clear expectations using:
    - Written procedures
    - Success metrics
    - Decision boundaries
    - Regular check-ins

- Permission to Fail Forward: Create an environment where:
    - Mistakes are learning opportunities
    - Innovation is rewarded
    - Questions are encouraged
    - Growth is celebrated

The Liberation Effect

The moment you truly start letting go, something remarkable happens. Your team steps up in ways you never imagined. They bring fresh perspectives, innovative solutions, and a level of ownership that transforms your business.

Remember: Your job isn't to do everything; it's to create an environment where everything can be done excellently without you.

Key Tools for Success

"What software should I use?"

This might be the question I get asked most often. While I love sharing our tech stack at KelliWorks, let me start with an important truth: The best tool isn't always the newest or the most expensive; it's the one you and your team will actually use.

Start With the Basics

Think of business software like building a house. You need a strong foundation before adding all the fancy features. Here's how we approach it at KelliWorks:

Core Operations

- A reliable accounting system
- Project management tools
- Communication platforms
- Document storage
- Time tracking

Don't feel pressured to implement everything at once. Remember, sophistication is often the enemy of execution.

The Smart Way to Choose Tools

Before jumping into any new software:

1. Identify the specific problem you're trying to solve.
2. Start with a free trial or demo.
3. Get your team's input.
4. Consider integration capabilities with your existing tools.

Pro Tip: Most software companies offer free training or onboarding support. Use it! That "free demo" isn't just a sales pitch; it's valuable training time.

Staying Current Without Getting Overwhelmed

Here's how to keep up with technology without losing your mind:

- Subscribe to 1–2 industry newsletters.
- Join relevant LinkedIn groups.
- Follow thought leaders in your field.
- Attend virtual demos quarterly.

But remember, just because something is new doesn't mean you need it. We evaluate new tools based on three criteria:

1. Will it save significant time?
2. Will it improve client experience?
3. Will the team actually use it?

Our Tested Tool Stack

Here's what works for us (your needs might be different):

Communication and Collaboration

- Slack for internal communication.

- Zoom for virtual meetings with AI meeting assistance.
- Dropbox or Google Workspace for document collaboration.

Project Management

- Asana or Trello for task management
- Monday.com for client projects
- Calendly for scheduling (seamless connection with CRM)

Financial Operations

- QuickBooks Online for accounting
- Bill.com/Ramp for payments
- Expensify for expense tracking

The Human Factor

The most sophisticated software won't help if your team isn't comfortable using it. To ensure seamless adoption, we:

- Include team members in software decisions.
- Allocate time for training.
- Create internal user guides.
- Celebrate software wins.

Remember, technology should serve your business, not the other way around. Start small, scale smart, and always prioritize usability over features.

The Mindset of Success

Let's talk about the most dangerous myth in business: glorification of the hustle.

You've seen the social media posts: "Rise and Grind," "Sleep When You're Dead," "24/7/365." I used to believe in this mentality. In fact, I wore my 80-hour workweeks like a badge of honor until my body and mind gave me a wake-up call that changed everything.

The Success Paradox

Here's what nobody tells you about success: Working longer hours doesn't equal better results. In fact, the opposite is often true. When I finally started prioritizing my well-being, something unexpected happened: my business actually grew faster.

Breaking Free From the Hustle Culture

The real breakthrough comes when you understand that:

- Exhaustion isn't a status symbol.
- Balance isn't a luxury.
- Rest is a business strategy.
- Boundaries create growth.

The New Success Metrics

At KelliWorks, we've redefined what success looks like:

- Instead of asking, "How many hours did you work?" we ask, "What impact did you make?"
- Instead of asking, "How busy are you?" we ask, "How effective are you?"
- Instead of asking, "Can you take on more?" we ask, "Is this the best use of your energy?"

Mindset-Shifting Exercises

- The Daily Reflection: Begin each day by asking yourself:
  - *What are my top three priorities for today?*
  - *How will I know that I've succeeded today?*
  - *What can I let go of to focus on what matters?*
- The Weekly Reset: Every week, take 30 minutes to reflect on:
- The Success Visualization: Spend 5 minutes visualizing your ideal work-life balance. Imagine what it looks like, what it feels like, and how it impacts your well-being. Use this vision to guide your decisions.
  - What worked well this week?
  - What drained my energy?
  - What will I do differently next week?

Wellness Practices for Business Growth

1. **Mindful Breaks:** Incorporate short, mindful breaks into your day. Use techniques such as deep breathing, stretching, or a quick walk to recharge.
2. **Digital Detox:** Set boundaries on screen time, especially before bed. Consider having a "tech-free" hour each evening to unwind.
3. **Movement as Medicine:** Regular physical activity boosts creativity and reduces stress. Whether it is yoga, running, or dancing, find what energizes you.
4. **Nourishment Over Nutrition:** Focus on eating foods that fuel both your body and mind. Listen to your body's needs and prioritize balanced meals.

The ROI of Well-Being

When you prioritize sustainability:

- Creativity flourishes
- Decision-making improves
- Team morale increases
- Client relationships deepen
- Innovation happens naturally

A Personal Note

I now measure my success not by the size of our revenue but by the quality of my life alongside that revenue. Can I attend my children's events? Do I have the energy for family dinners? Am I present in my relationships? These aren't just personal metrics; they're indicators of business success.

Remember, your business should support your life, not consume it.

Making the Shift: Small Changes That Lead to Big Transformations

Every great transformation begins with a single step. The journey to a collaborative and efficient business does not require a complete overhaul overnight. Instead, it is about making small, intentional changes that compound over time to create a significant impact.

1. **Start with One Process:** Choose one process in your business that feels cumbersome or outdated. It might be your client onboarding, billing, or reporting. Focus on streamlining this one area first. Document it, automate what you can, and delegate the rest. Celebrate the success before moving on to the next.

2. **Set Clear Intentions:** Before diving into new strategies, take a moment to set clear intentions for your business. Ask yourself:
   - *What do I want my business to look like in one year?*
   - *How do I want my team to feel while working here?*
   - *What impact do I want to have on my clients?*
3. **Foster a Culture of Collaboration:** Encourage open communication and idea-sharing within your team. Create regular opportunities for collaboration, whether through team meetings, brainstorming sessions, or informal check-ins. Remember, the best ideas often come from unexpected places.
4. **Embrace Continuous Learning:** Stay curious and open to new ideas. Encourage your team to do the same. Invest in training, attend workshops, and explore new technologies that can enhance your business operations. Remember, growth is a journey, not a destination.
5. **Reflect and Adjust:** Regularly take time to reflect on what is working and what is not. Be willing to adjust your strategies as needed. Flexibility and adaptability are key to long-term success.

Seeking Professional Guidance

As you navigate these changes, keep in mind that you don't have to do it alone. If you ever feel lost or overwhelmed, consider hiring professionals who can provide guidance and expertise. Trust that by investing in the right support, you are sowing the seeds of success in your business. This trust and belief in your vision will ultimately lead to reaping the rewards of your efforts.

Recommended Professionals and Resources for Small Businesses

- Business Coaches: Helping you refine your strategy and grow with confidence.
- Accountants: Ensuring your financial health and compliance.
- Legal Advisors: Protecting your business and navigating complex regulations.
- Marketing Experts: Effectively reaching and engaging your target audience.
- IT Specialists: Implementing preventative measures to safeguard your technology and data.
- Insurance Brokers: Even work-from-home businesses need insurance to protect against unforeseen risks.

Setting Intentions for a Collaborative and Efficient Business

As you make these shifts, keep your intentions front and center:

- Prioritize well-being alongside productivity.
- Foster a supportive, collaborative team environment.
- Embrace technology as a tool for empowerment, not overwhelm.
- Focus on creating value, not just revenue.

By making these intentional changes, you're not just transforming your business; you're creating a legacy of sustainable success.

Remember: The most successful businesses aren't built overnight; they're built one thoughtful decision at a time.

CHAPTER 3

THE FREEDOM FRAMEWORK

Remember when we talked about that business owner spending 8 to 10 hours on payroll? That's a perfect example of what happens without proper systems in place. The Freedom Framework isn't just another business methodology; it's your escape plan from being trapped in day-to-day operations.

Think of it as building a self-driving car for your business. Just as you wouldn't want to manually control every aspect of driving, you shouldn't need to manually handle every aspect of your business. The Framework provides the "autopilot" systems that allow your business to run smoothly while you focus on navigation and your destination.

What Is the Freedom Framework?

The Concept of a Business That Runs Without You

Imagine waking up tomorrow knowing your business will generate revenue whether you show up or not. Not because you've hired a replacement for yourself, but because you've built something more valuable, a business that operates on systems rather than heroics.

The Freedom Framework isn't about working harder or even smarter in the conventional sense. It's about fundamentally shifting how you think about your business. Instead of seeing yourself as the central gear that keeps everything turning, you become the architect who designs a machine that runs smoothly with minimal intervention.

I discovered this concept through necessity rather than brilliance. After the incidents I told you about (pumping milk between client meetings and missing my son's early milestones), I realized something had to change. I couldn't keep being the center of everything. My business needed to work without me for both my sanity and its sustainability.

What does a business that runs without you actually look like in practice? It's when:

- Clients receive consistent, high-quality service regardless of who delivers it.
- New team members can become productive quickly by following established processes.
- Problems are solved using systems rather than requiring your personal attention.
- Growth doesn't mean proportionally more work for you.

- You can take a vacation, a real one, and return to a business that's thriving.

Why Systems Are the Key to Freedom

Here's the truth that transformed my business: Systems are the only path to sustainable freedom. Not hiring more people, not working longer hours, and not even delegating better, but systems.

Why? Because without systems:

- Knowledge stays trapped in people's heads (especially yours).
- Quality depends on individual effort rather than standardized processes.
- Scaling means more chaos, not more revenue.
- Your business becomes vulnerable to turnover and absences.
- Growth hits a ceiling, the limit of your personal capacity.

Systems create freedom through predictability. When you know exactly how things should work, when they should happen, and who should handle them, you eliminate the chaos that keeps pulling you back into daily operations.

Think about McDonald's for a moment. Love it or hate it, their founder, Ray Kroc, built the ultimate system-based business. A teenager in Tokyo can deliver the same experience as one in Toronto because they're following the same precise systems. The business runs without the founder; in fact, it runs without any single person being essential.

Your business may never be McDonald's, but the principle remains the same: your freedom is directly proportional to the quality of your systems. In the coming sections, we'll explore exactly how to build these systems for your unique business.

The Pillars of the Freedom Framework

The Freedom Framework stands on three essential pillars that work together to create a business that can operate without your constant involvement. These aren't just nice-to-have improvements. They're the fundamental building blocks of a business designed for freedom.

Standardizing Processes for Consistency

When I first started standardizing processes at Kelli-Works, I faced serious resistance, mostly from myself. "Every client is different," I would argue. "We need to be flexible." Does that sound familiar?

But here's what I discovered: Standardization doesn't mean treating every situation identically. It means creating a consistent approach that delivers reliable results while allowing for necessary customization.

Effective standardization begins with identifying your core processes, the activities that occur repeatedly in your business. For us, these included client onboarding, monthly financial reviews, tax preparation, and client communication.

We mapped each process step by step, identifying:

- Exactly what happens at each stage.
- Who is responsible for each action.
- What the expected outcome looks like.
- Where customization is appropriate.
- How to handle exceptions.

The magic happens when you transform these processes from tribal knowledge into documented systems. We created what we call "Process Playbooks", visual guides that anyone can follow to deliver consistent results. These aren't stuffy procedural manuals; they're practical tools with checklists, templates, and clear decision points.

The result? A new team member can now deliver the same quality of service as someone who has been with us for years. Clients receive consistent experiences regardless of who serves them. And perhaps most importantly, these standards become the baseline for continuous improvement.

Automating Repetitive Tasks

After standardizing, automation follows, replacing human effort with technology for repetitive, predictable tasks. This isn't about replacing people; it's about freeing their time for higher-value work.

Start by asking, "What tasks are we doing repeatedly that don't require human judgment?" For us, these included:

- Sending reminder emails for missing documents
- Generating standard reports
- Moving data between systems
- Scheduling follow-up communications
- Creating recurring calendar appointments

By leveraging AI or using tools like Zapier, Microsoft Power Automate, and industry-specific software, we created automation workflows that handle these tasks without human intervention. One example is when a client uploads a tax document to our portal. The system automatically categorizes it, notifies the appropriate team member, updates our tracking dashboard, and sends the client a confirmation, all without anyone lifting a finger.

The productivity gains have been extraordinary. Tasks that once consumed hours now occur in the background while we focus on work that truly requires our expertise and attention.

Delegating Responsibilities Effectively

The final pillar, and often the most challenging, is effective delegation. Even with standardized processes and automation, certain tasks will always require human judgment and attention. The key is ensuring that they do not all require *your* judgment and attention.

Effective delegation in the Freedom Framework goes beyond simply assigning tasks; it involves creating a structured approach to decision-making and responsibility. We have developed what we call "Decision Matrices," clear guidelines that empower team members to handle situations independently while knowing exactly when to escalate.

For example, our client services team has a matrix that outlines:

- What they can decide independently (adjusting deadlines within certain parameters).
- What requires team lead approval (fee adjustments under a specific threshold).
- What needs director input (changing service scope).
- What must come to me (strategic account decisions).

This approach fosters confidence on both sides. Team members know they will not be criticized for making decisions within their authority, and I know that important matters will reach me while routine issues are handled appropriately.

Together, these three pillars, standardization, automation, and delegation, create the foundation for a business that operates without your constant presence. They transform your role from operator to owner, from doer to leader, and from bottleneck to visionary.

In the next section, we will explore how to implement these pillars by creating operational systems for specific areas of your business.

Building a Self-Sufficient Team

The systems and technology we've discussed are powerful, but they are just tools. It is your team that brings them to life. Building a self-sufficient team is not just about hiring talented people; it is about creating an environment where they can thrive independently within your systems.

Training and Empowering Your Team to Follow Systems

When I first started implementing systems at KelliWorks, I made a critical mistake. I built elaborate processes and then simply handed them over to my team with a cheerful, "Here you go!" The result? Confusion, resistance, and systems that existed only on paper or in the cloud.

I have learned that effective system adoption requires a thoughtful approach to training and empowerment.

Start With the Why

People resist systems they do not understand. Before introducing any new process, explain:

- Why it matters to the business.
- How it benefits clients.
- What problems it solves.
- How it makes their work more meaningful.

When our team understood that our new project management system was not about monitoring their work but about eliminating the bottlenecks that frustrated them daily, resistance melted away.

Build System Champions

Identify team members who naturally embrace systems and empower them to become internal advocates. At KelliWorks, we created "System Champions" for each department, team members who receive advanced training and serve as the first point of contact for questions.

These champions help train new team members, provide feedback on system improvements, and bridge the gap between leadership vision and frontline implementation.

They are not managers, but they are recognized and rewarded for their system expertise.

Create Layered Learning Experiences

Different people learn differently, and complex systems require multiple exposure points. Our training approach now includes:

- Interactive workshops for initial system introduction.
- Written documentation for reference.
- Video tutorials for visual learners.
- Support for AI integrations.
- Shadowing opportunities with experienced team members.
- Guided practice with real scenarios.
- Refresher sessions for ongoing reinforcement.

This layered approach ensures that team members not only understand how to follow the systems but also why each step matters.

Balance Structure with Autonomy

The most effective systems provide clear guardrails while allowing for professional judgment. When training your team, explicitly identify:

- Non-negotiable elements that must be followed exactly.

- Areas where they can (and should) apply their expertise.
- Decision points where they have the authority to choose the path forward.

For example, our client communication system specifies exactly when clients should receive updates (non-negotiable) but empowers team members to personalize the content based on the client relationship (autonomy).

Encouraging Initiative and Accountability

A truly self-sufficient team doesn't just follow systems; they improve them. They take ownership of results, not just tasks. Here's how we foster this mindset.

Create Safe Spaces for Innovation

We established regular "System Innovation Sessions" where team members can suggest improvements to existing processes. These aren't just suggestion boxes; they're structured discussions with clear paths to implementation. The rule is simple: If you identify a problem with a system, come prepared with a potential solution. This shifts the culture from complaint to contribution. Some of our most valuable process improvements have come from team members who use the systems daily.

Implement Clear Accountability Structures

Freedom requires accountability, not micromanagement. For each key system, we've defined:

- What success looks like (specific, measurable outcomes).
- Who's responsible for each component.
- How and when progress will be measured.
- What happens when targets are missed.

When everyone understands what's expected and how it will be measured, they can take ownership of their results. Our monthly team dashboards show system performance metrics, creating healthy transparency and allowing everyone to see how their work contributes to the whole.

Reward System Adoption and Improvement

We actively recognize and reward behaviors that strengthen our systems. This includes:

- Team members who consistently follow processes.
- Those who identify system weaknesses.
- People who develop creative solutions.
- Departments that achieve efficiency milestones.

These aren't just symbolic gestures. Our bonus structure includes components tied to system adherence and improvement. What gets rewarded gets repeated.

Build a Culture of Continuous Learning

Self-sufficiency requires continuous growth. We invest in our team's development through:

- Regular training on system updates.
- Cross-training to build broader understanding.
- Industry education to keep skills current.
- Leadership development for rising system champions.

When team members grow, their capacity to work independently within the systems also increases.

The ultimate test of a self-sufficient team comes when you step away. Fifteen years into the business, I was finally able to take a three-week vacation completely disconnected from everything. No email, no check-ins, no emergency line. I returned to find that not only had everything continued smoothly, but the team had also implemented two system improvements in my absence.

That's when I knew we had truly built something special: a team that doesn't just operate within the Freedom Framework but actively strengthens it.

Measuring Success

"What gets measured gets managed."

Peter Drucker's famous words have become a business cliché, but they are at the heart of the Freedom Framework. Without clear metrics, you cannot know if your systems are actually creating the freedom you designed them for.

Tracking System Performance and Efficiency

When I first implemented systems at KelliWorks, I made a rookie mistake: I focused exclusively on financial metrics. Revenue was up, so the systems must be working, right? Not necessarily. I soon discovered that while we were making more money, our team was working longer hours, clients were waiting longer for responses, and I was still caught up in daily operations.

True system success requires a more nuanced measurement approach.

The Freedom Metrics Dashboard

We developed what we call our "Freedom Metrics Dashboard," a comprehensive view of system performance across four key dimensions:

1. **Efficiency Metrics:** How well are our systems optimizing resources?
    - Time spent per deliverable

  - Processing cycle time (how long work takes from start to finish)
  - Resource utilization rates
  - Rework percentage (how often things need correction)
  - Automation ratio (percentage of tasks handled without human intervention)

2. **Quality Metrics:** Are our systems delivering consistent excellence?
   - Error rates
   - Client satisfaction scores
   - Adherence to standards
   - First-time completion rates
   - Quality audit results
3. **Team Impact Metrics:** How are systems affecting our people?
   - Team satisfaction scores
   - Overtime hours
   - System adoption rates
   - Cross-training progress
   - Innovation suggestions submitted and implemented

4. **Owner Freedom Metrics:** Is the business actually running without you?
    - Owner involvement in operational decisions
    - True time off (completely disconnected from the business)
    - Strategic planning time
    - Revenue per owner hour
    - Sleep quality (yes, we actually track this!)

We review these metrics monthly, looking not just at the numbers themselves but also at the trends and relationships between them. This comprehensive view prevents the common trap of optimizing one area at the expense of others.

Leading vs. Lagging Indicators

One crucial distinction we've learned to make is between leading and lagging indicators.

Lagging indicators show results after they have occurred: revenue, profit margins, and client retention. These indicators tell you if your systems worked in the past.

Leading indicators predict future success: system adoption rates, process compliance, and team capability scores. These indicators tell you if your systems will work going forward.

A balanced measurement approach includes both. For example, we track not only client satisfaction (lagging) but also adherence to our client communication protocol (leading), knowing that consistent communication today predicts satisfied clients tomorrow.

Adjusting and Improving Processes Over Time

Measurement without adjustment is merely scorekeeping. The real power of the Freedom Framework comes from using metrics to drive continuous improvement.

The System Maturity Model

Not all systems require the same level of sophistication. We use a four-stage maturity model to guide our improvement efforts.

Stage 1: Defined—The process is documented and followed consistently, but it may still be largely manual and require significant oversight.

Stage 2: Managed—The process has clear metrics, standardized tools, and dedicated ownership. Variations are controlled and understood.

Stage 3: Optimized—The process incorporates automation, integrates with other systems, and requires minimal oversight. Continuous improvement mechanisms are in place.

Stage 4: Transformative—The process delivers a strategic advantage, adapts automatically to changing conditions, and generates insights that drive business growth.

Each key system in our business has a current maturity rating and a target. We focus our improvement efforts on advancing systems to their appropriate target level. Not every process needs to reach Stage 4.

Remember: The goal isn't perfect systems; it's systems that perfectly support your vision of freedom. Some processes might remain relatively simple if they are not critical to your core operations or freedom goals. The true mark of success isn't just having metrics and reviews. It's developing an organizational mindset that sees systems as living assets to be nurtured and evolved. When your team automatically thinks, "How could we improve this?" rather than just "How do we do this?" that's when the Freedom Framework truly takes root.

Prioritizing Systems to Implement Now

With your assessment complete, it's time to identify where to focus first. The key is to start with systems that create the biggest impact with the least resistance.

The Impact-Effort Matrix

Create a simple four-quadrant matrix:

- X-axis: Implementation Effort (Low to High)
- Y-axis: Freedom Impact (Low to High)

Plot your potential system improvements on this matrix. Focus first on the High Impact/Low Effort quadrant, the "quick wins" that will build momentum and demonstrate the value of the Freedom Framework.

Start With These Three Systems

Based on my experience with hundreds of business owners, these three systems almost always belong in the high-impact, relatively low-effort category:

1. **Client Communication System**
    - Document standard client touchpoints.
    - Create templates for routine communications.
    - Establish response time standards.
    - Implement a shared inbox or client portal.
    - Define escalation paths for complex issues.

    This system often creates immediate relief because client communication tends to be one of the biggest drains on owner time.

2. **Meeting Management System**
    - Create standard agendas for recurring meetings.
    - Implement preparation and follow-up protocols.
    - Define clear decision-making processes.
    - Document meeting roles and responsibilities.
    - Establish timeboxing for efficient discussions.

    Meetings are notorious time-wasters. A structured system can reclaim hours of productive time each week.

3. **Basic Project Management System**
    - Identify your core service delivery processes.
    - Document key milestones and deliverables.
    - Create standard workflows for common projects.
    - Implement simple task management tools.
    - Establish clear handoff procedures between team members.

    This system addresses the fundamental question: "How does work move through our business?"

The 30-60-90 Day Freedom Plan

With your priority systems identified, create a phased implementation plan.

First 30 Days

- Document one core process each week.
- Implement basic versions of your priority systems.
- Train your team on the fundamentals of the systems.
- Set baseline metrics to track improvements.

Days 31–60

- Refine systems based on initial feedback.
- Add automation to repetitive processes.
- Expand systems to cover additional scenarios.
- Implement regular system review meetings.

Days 61–90

- Integrate the systems with one another.
- Develop more sophisticated metrics.
- Build accountability structures within the team.
- Plan your first “system test” by stepping back from daily operations.

Remember: Progress Over Perfection

The biggest barrier to freedom isn't poor systems; it's the pursuit of perfect systems. Start simple. Document what you're already doing. Improve incrementally. A basic system that everyone follows is infinitely better than a sophisticated system that exists only in concept.

As one of my clients put it: "I spent years thinking about creating systems someday when I had time. Now I realize that creating systems is what gives me time."

Your business can run without you. Not perfectly at first, not completely, but enough to give you breathing room. Enough to help you rediscover why you started this journey. Enough to let you build something truly extraordinary, a business that serves your life rather than a life that serves your business.

The Freedom Framework isn't just about work. It's about reclaiming the freedom that inspired you to become an entrepreneur in the first place. And it starts with a single step: deciding that freedom matters enough to build systems that support it. Where will you begin?

CHAPTER 4

THE TEAM TRANSFORM

You've built the systems, established the processes, and implemented the technology. Yet something is still missing. That's because the final piece of your freedom puzzle isn't found in software or flowcharts. It's in the people who bring your business to life.

The journey begins long before you have a full team. As a solopreneur, that critical moment arrives when you realize you can't do it all yourself anymore. This first hire might be an employee or a contractor, a decision that shapes your early team culture. While contractors offer flexibility, employees often bring a level of dedication and investment that can transform your business from the ground up.

The traditional entrepreneurial narrative celebrates the lone visionary making all the decisions. But here's what I've learned through years of trial and error: Your greatest leverage comes not from controlling every aspect of your business but from creating a team environment where everyone contributes their best, whether that's your first virtual assistant or a department of specialists.

In this chapter, we'll explore how to transform your team from dependent executors into collaborative partners, the shift that finally allows your business to thrive without your constant presence.

From Dictatorship to Collaboration

Back when I had just purchased my first home, a major milestone for me as a single mom and entrepreneur, I was still operating like a one-woman band at KelliWorks. I had help, technically. A part-time assistant who would work "whenever she was free" after her full-time job. In reality, it felt like I was constantly begging her to finish tasks, always walking on eggshells because she was "doing me a favor."

Even after signing my mortgage on closing day, I still mentally triple-checked every client file and every payroll report late into the night. I used to joke that I wasn't just the CEO. I was the "unofficial last line of defense."

One day, sitting in my new living room, I thought about turning my first-floor sitting area into an office. I found myself wandering into the Container Store, daydreaming about desks and file cabinets. But deep down, I knew I needed more than just furniture.

That's when everything shifted. I met my first business coach, the first person who asked me a question powerful enough to make me *dream*. He asked:

> "What do you really want for your business?"

For the first time, I said it out loud:

> "I want an office. I want a real team. I want to teach someone how to work the KelliWorks way."

From there, things started aligning like magic. I accidentally sent an email to the wrong person, who replied, asking about my services. We met for coffee, and that "wrong email" led to the highest-paying client referral I had ever received. Suddenly, I had a new client, a new office space, and the chance to hire my first real team member. But trust me, it didn't come wrapped in a bow. The self-doubt hit hard: "Who do you think you are, Kelli? You just bought a house. Now you think you can afford an office?"

When I found the woman I wanted to hire, she asked for a salary that, at the time, felt huge to me. I won't even put the real number here. It was *humble* by business standards, but for me then, it was terrifying. Paying her weekly would stretch me beyond what I had. But deep inside, I knew that if I wanted to grow, I couldn't afford **not** to invest in help.

I chose to trust that if I took the leap, even scraping from Peter to pay Paul, **good would come from it**. That very first week, I could already feel the difference between hiring an employee who was *invested* in our mission and a part-timer doing me a favor.

On her very first day, while training her on a process workaround I had rigged up (like so many small business owners do), she looked at me innocently and said: "Why don't we just fix the problem instead of working around it?" That one sentence stopped me cold. In that moment, for the first time, **I felt supported inside my business**. Someone wasn't just doing a task; they were thinking alongside me. They cared about doing it better. They cared about **us** succeeding.

And it clicked: "True leadership isn't about catching every ball. It's about building people who catch their own, and sometimes throw better than you ever could."

The Benefits of Building a Collaborative Team Environment

The transition from dictatorship to collaboration didn't happen overnight at KelliWorks. It required intentional changes and, honestly, some uncomfortable self-reflection. However, the benefits became apparent quickly:

Enhanced Retention and Recruitment

The shift dramatically improved our ability to retain and attract talent. Exit interviews consistently cited "limited growth opportunities" and "lack of autonomy" as reasons for departure. After implementing collaborative practices, our retention rate improved by 65%, and candidates began specifically mentioning our "team culture" as a reason for wanting to join us.

Perhaps most importantly for business owners seeking freedom, collaboration builds leadership capacity throughout the organization. Team members develop decision-making skills, strategic thinking, and problem-solving abilities, essentially learning to think like owners. This creates a pipeline of capable leaders who can step up when you step back.

Greater Business Resilience

A collaborative team is more adaptable to market changes and challenges. When COVID-19 hit, we didn't have to wait for me to develop our remote work strategy. Our team quickly assembled, evaluated options, and implemented solutions, many of which I wouldn't have thought of myself.

The transformation from dictatorship to collaboration doesn't mean abdicating your vision or authority. You're still the owner and the ultimate decision-maker on crucial matters. However, it does mean creating space for others to contribute meaningfully to how that vision comes to life.

In my experience, this shift is less about grand gestures and more about daily practices: asking instead of telling, listening before deciding, celebrating independent thinking, and being willing to implement ideas that aren't your own.

The most powerful question I learned to ask my team was, "What do you think we should do here?" And the most powerful thing I learned to do after asking was to actually listen to the answer.

Empowering Your Dream Team

Identifying and Leveraging Individual Strengths

A crucial insight changed everything about how I built teams. People perform exponentially better when working from their strengths rather than struggling to overcome weaknesses.

When I started KelliWorks, I hired for technical skills and then expected everyone to perform equally across all aspects of the job. Our bookkeepers needed to manage client relationships, handle detailed reconciliations, and create financial reports, regardless of their natural aptitudes. The result? Mediocrity across the board, as team members struggled with tasks that drained their energy.

The turning point came when I noticed something obvious in retrospect. Sarah, who struggled with detailed reconciliations, excelled at client communication. Mean-while, Michael, who avoided client calls whenever possible, could spot patterns in financial data with remarkable precision. They were both trying to be well-rounded, and both felt like they were failing.

Here's the systematic approach we now use to identify and leverage individual strengths:

Strengths Discovery Process

1. **Formal Assessment:** We use tools like Clifton-Strengths (formerly StrengthsFinder) and DISC profiles to identify each team member's natural talents and work preferences. These are not personality tests; they are practical tools that reveal how people naturally think, feel, and behave.
2. **Performance Pattern Analysis:** We review past work to identify where each person has excelled naturally. What projects energized them? Where have they gone above and beyond expectations? Where have they struggled despite their best efforts?
3. **Career Conversation:** Perhaps most importantly, we simply ask team members, "What parts of your work make you feel strong? When do you lose track of time because you are so engaged? What tasks do you look forward to?"
4. **Peer Feedback:** Often, others see strengths that we do not recognize in ourselves. We gather input from colleagues about where each team member makes their greatest contributions.

Strength Deployment Strategy

Once we understand individual strengths, we redesign roles and responsibilities accordingly:

1. **Strength-Aligned Responsibilities:** We assign primary responsibilities that align with core strengths. Sarah now leads client interactions and training, while Michael focuses on complex reconciliations and financial analysis.
2. **Complementary Partnerships:** We create teams where members' strengths complement each other. Instead of everyone doing everything, we pair people whose abilities fill each other's gaps.
3. **Strength-Based Development:** Rather than focusing primarily on fixing weaknesses, we invest in helping people become exceptional in their areas of natural talent. This doesn't mean ignoring development needs, but it does mean putting most of our energy where there is the greatest potential for excellence.
4. **Project Assignments:** We assign special projects and initiatives based on strengths rather than availability or seniority. This ensures we achieve the best possible outcomes while giving team members opportunities to shine.

The results have been remarkable: Productivity is up by 47%, team satisfaction has increased by 34%, and client feedback consistently highlights the exceptional quality of our work. Most importantly, team members report feeling "in their element" rather than constantly struggling against their natural wiring.

Encouraging Team Members to Take Ownership

Identifying strengths is just the first step. The real transformation occurs when team members shift from seeing themselves as employees following directions to owners responsible for outcomes. This ownership mindset is the secret ingredient that allows your business to thrive without your constant presence.

Here's how we foster this mindset at KelliWorks:

The Authority-Responsibility Balance

The fundamental principle is that authority should match responsibility. We found that team members wouldn't take true ownership when they were responsible for outcomes but lacked the authority to make decisions. Conversely, granting authority without clear responsibility created chaos.

Our solution was to create what we call "Ownership Domains," clearly defined areas where team members have both the responsibility for results and the authority to determine how to achieve them.

For example, our client onboarding specialist doesn't just execute a checklist I created; she owns the entire onboarding experience, with the authority to modify processes, create resources, and make decisions that ensure new clients have a seamless transition into our service.

Creating a Culture of Accountability

Accountability often gets a bad rap, conjured as a stern taskmaster tracking every move. However, true accountability isn't about micromanagement or punitive measures. It's about creating clarity and commitment that empower your team to deliver their best work consistently.

Setting Clear Expectations and Goals

The foundation of accountability is crystal-clear expectations. I learned this lesson the hard way when a project went sideways, and a team member said, "I thought I was doing exactly what you wanted." The painful truth? She was right. My instructions had been vague, leaving her to guess my expectations.

At KelliWorks, we now use a structured approach to setting expectations.

The CLEAR method ensures every team member understands exactly what success looks like:

- **Context:** Why this matters to the business and clients.

- **Limitations:** Boundaries, budget constraints, and non-negotiables.
- **Expectations:** Specific deliverables and quality standards.
- **Authority:** Decisions they can make independently.
- **Results:** How outcomes will be measured.

For ongoing responsibilities, we create Role Clarity Documents that outline primary accountabilities, key performance indicators, and decision-making authority. These are not static job descriptions, but living agreements that evolve as team members grow.

For projects and initiatives, we use Outcome-Based Planning rather than task-based delegation. Instead of prescribing exact steps, we define the desired outcome and success criteria, then allow team members to determine how to achieve them.

The key insight? When expectations are crystal clear, accountability becomes self-directed rather than imposed. Team members can evaluate their own performance against agreed-upon standards rather than waiting for your assessment.

Establishing Transparent Communication Practices

Clear expectations provide the foundation, but accountability thrives on transparent communication. We have implemented several practices that maintain visibility without creating a culture of surveillance:

Regular Rhythm of Accountability: We maintain a consistent cadence of check-ins at different levels:

- Daily stand-up meetings (15 minutes) for tactical coordination.
- Weekly team huddles (45 minutes) for progress updates and obstacle removal.
- Monthly strategy sessions (90 minutes) for reviewing metrics and adjusting plans.

Visibility Systems: We have created dashboards that provide real-time visibility into key performance indicators for each role and project. These are not used as surveillance tools but as feedback mechanisms that help team members self-correct before small issues become major problems.

The No-Surprise Rule: This simple principle has transformed our communication culture. No one should ever be surprised during a performance review. Feedback is delivered in real time, both positive and constructive, creating a continuous improvement loop rather than periodic judgment.

Structured Problem-Solving: When things go off track, we avoid blame and focus on solutions using our "Four A" process:

- **Acknowledge** the issue without blame or excuses.
- **Analyze** what happened and why.
- **Adjust** the approach based on learnings.
- **Advance** with the improved solution.

This accountability framework creates an environment where transparency is valued over perfection. Team members know it is better to raise issues early than to hide challenges until they become crises. They take ownership of their results because they have the clarity, support, and communication channels needed to succeed.

The ultimate measure of effective accountability? When it shifts from being externally enforced to internally embraced, when your team holds themselves to high standards not because you are watching, but because they are committed to excellence and have the clarity to achieve it.

Fostering Innovation and Initiative

A business that can truly run without you needs more than team members who follow systems. It requires people who think creatively, solve problems independently, and continuously improve how things work. Without innovation and initiative, even the best systems eventually become outdated or irrelevant.

Encouraging Creativity and Problem-Solving Within the Team

At KelliWorks, we discovered that innovation doesn't just happen spontaneously; it requires intentional cultivation. The turning point came when I realized I was unintentionally shutting down creative thinking by having an immediate answer for everything. Team members stopped bringing ideas because I always had a solution ready.

We transformed our approach with these practical strategies:

The Questions-First Rule: Leadership team members commit to responding to problems with questions rather than immediate solutions. Instead of saying, "Here's what you should do," we ask, "What approaches have you considered?" This simple shift signals that thinking is valued over compliance.

Innovation Time: We allocate 10% of each team member's schedule to improvement projects of their choosing. This dedicated space for creativity has yielded some of our most valuable process improvements, including an automated reporting system that saves 15 hours monthly.

Problem-Solving Framework: We've equipped the team with a consistent methodology for tackling challenges:

- Define the real problem (not just symptoms).
- Generate multiple possible solutions.
- Evaluate options against clear criteria.
- Implement, measure, and refine.

Cross-Functional Collaboration: Some of our best innovations come from unexpected perspectives. Our monthly "Fresh Eyes" sessions bring together team members from different departments to examine processes from new angles. When our administrative assistant reviewed our client onboarding process, she identified simplifications that had eluded our specialists.

Overcoming Challenges in Team Dynamics

The shift from dictatorship to collaboration isn't always smooth sailing. Even the most promising team transformations encounter obstacles, and how you navigate these challenges often determines whether your collaborative culture thrives or falters.

Addressing Resistance to Change

When we began transforming KelliWorks' team culture, I was surprised to discover that not everyone embraced the changes with open arms. Some team members actually preferred the old top-down approach; it was familiar, predictable, and required less personal responsibility.

We've developed a practical approach to addressing resistance:

- **Understand the Source:** Resistance typically stems from one of three concerns: competence ("I don't know how to work this way"), control ("I'm comfortable with the current process"), or clarity ("I don't understand why we're changing"). Identifying the specific concern allows for targeted support.
- **Personalize the Transition:** Some team members need detailed guidance and frequent reassurance, while others prefer space to adapt at their own pace. We create individualized transition plans rather than forcing a one-size-fits-all approach.
- **Focus on Early Wins:** We identify opportunities for quick, visible successes that demonstrate the benefits of the new approach. These early wins build momentum and convert skeptics more effectively than any amount of theoretical explanation.
- **Honor the Past:** Acknowledging the value of previous contributions prevents defensive reactions. Rather than positioning changes as corrections to "wrong" approaches, we frame them as evolutions that build on past successes.

Navigating Conflicts and Maintaining a Positive Culture

Collaborative environments do not eliminate conflict; they transform how it is handled. At KelliWorks, we have found that healthy disagreement is actually essential for innovation, but it requires the right framework to be productive.

Our conflict navigation approach includes:

- **The Disagreement Protocol:** We have established a simple structure for productive conflict: state your perspective, explain your reasoning, listen to understand (not to respond), identify points of agreement, and collaborate on resolving differences. This protocol prevents disagreements from becoming personal.
- **Address Issues Early:** We follow the "one conversation" rule, address concerns directly with the involved person before discussing them with others. This prevents the destructive spiral of triangulation and gossip that can poison team culture.
- **Focus on Shared Purpose:** When conflicts arise, we reconnect to our common goals and values. Reminding everyone that we are on the same team with shared objectives often defuses tension and reframes the discussion.

- **Culture Guardians:** We have identified and empowered team members who naturally embody our collaborative values to help maintain a positive environment. These informal leaders model constructive behaviors and gently redirect negativity.

Transforming team dynamics is not a one-time event but an ongoing journey. By anticipating challenges, addressing resistance with empathy, and creating frameworks for productive conflict, you build a resilient collaborative culture that can weather the inevitable storms of business growth.

Steps to Begin the Team Transformation

Even when the money wasn't there, I bet on myself and on my vision. I trusted that if I built a real team, *the dream would follow*. Despite scraping resources together in those early days, it worked. **Eleven years later**, I can proudly say:

- Payroll has never failed.
- My employees have always been supported.

And I learned early:

> "If you take care of your team, they'll take care of your clients."

That shift, from micromanaging to empowering, was the foundation of KelliWorks' freedom, growth, and the community we serve today.

Delegation isn't surrender; it's strategy, leadership, and freedom.

The journey from dictatorship to collaboration doesn't require a dramatic organizational overhaul. In fact, sudden, sweeping changes often backfire, creating resistance and confusion. Instead, successful transformations occur through intentional, incremental shifts that gradually reshape your team culture.

Assessing Your Current Team Structure and Dynamics

Before making changes, take the time to understand where you truly stand today. At KelliWorks, we began with a straightforward assessment that revealed insights we hadn't expected:

The Team Dynamic Audit: Conduct an honest evaluation of your current situation:

- How are decisions currently made? Who has input?
- Where do team members show initiative, and where do they wait for direction?
- What happens when mistakes occur? How do people respond?

- Who speaks in meetings, and who remains silent?
- What informal power structures exist beyond the organizational chart?

Feedback Collection: Create safe channels for team members to share their perspectives:

- Anonymous surveys about decision-making and collaboration.
- One-on-one conversations with a focus on listening.
- Team retrospectives on recent projects or challenges.

Self-Reflection: As the leader, honestly examine your own behaviors:

- How often do you override team decisions?
- Do you ask for input before sharing your opinion?
- How do you respond when team members disagree with you?
- What signals (intentional or not) do you send about autonomy?

This assessment often reveals surprising patterns. We discovered that our formal policies encouraged collaboration, but my habit of jumping in with solutions undermined team initiative behind the scenes.

Implementing Small Changes to Shift Toward Collaboration

With a clear understanding of your starting point, begin implementing targeted changes that shift dynamics without creating upheaval.

Start with Process, Not People: Begin by modifying how work is conducted rather than criticizing current behaviors. We introduced a simple rule that every proposed solution requires two alternatives before making a decision, naturally creating space for more voices.

Introduce Decision Clarity: Clearly designate which decisions are:

- Consultative (you will get input but make the final call)
- Collaborative (the team decides together)
- Delegated (specific individuals have full authority) This clarity prevents confusion about expectations.

Create Psychological Safety: Team members will not contribute if they fear negative consequences. Start by responding positively to input, especially when you disagree. We instituted a "no-penalty brainstorming" rule where all ideas receive consideration without immediate judgment.

Modify Meeting Structures: Meetings often reflect and reinforce power dynamics. Simple changes, such as rotating meeting facilitation, implementing round-robin input, or starting with team updates rather than leader pronouncements, can shift participation patterns.

Build Collaborative Habits: Introduce practices that gradually build collaborative skills:

- Start meetings by explicitly inviting input from quieter team members.
- Delay giving your opinion until others have spoken.
- Recognize and celebrate instances of team initiative.
- Follow up on suggestions, even if they are not implemented.

CHAPTER 5

LIFE-BUSINESS HARMONY

There's a particular kind of gut punch you never forget. For me, it came when I checked my Uber Eats app and saw it: **$1,100** spent in a single month. At first, I laughed; that dry, hollow kind of laugh that covers up the panic.

Then came the sinking feeling. The shame.

I wasn't buying designer bags or luxury trips. I wasn't even "living large." I was surviving. When the bank finally closed my personal account due to repeated overdrafts, I sat there confused because I hadn't been *buying* anything extravagant. But the receipts told the real story. I was using food delivery to *fuel my functioning depression.*

The bank allowed temporary overdrafts as long as I replenished them within a few days. **I had built my life on workarounds.** Workarounds for bad choices. Workarounds for exhaustion. Workarounds for a business that looked successful from the outside, but was hollowing me out from the inside. It wasn't about the food. It wasn't about the money. It was a receipt for the life I didn't want anymore. I had become the brokest (and heaviest) I had ever been. Running faster. Earning more. Breaking down harder. The truth hit hard: my so-called "success" was costing me my health, my peace, and my soul.

The Myth of Work-Life Balance

Why Balance Feels Impossible for Entrepreneurs

Let's address the elephant in the room: traditional work-life balance is a myth for entrepreneurs. The image of perfectly equal time devoted to work and personal life isn't just unrealistic; it's fundamentally misaligned with the entrepreneurial journey.

I spent years chasing this elusive balance, beating myself up for failing to achieve it. I would block off family time, only to have a client emergency derail my plans. I would schedule "me time," then surrender it to a pressing deadline. Sound familiar?

The truth is that entrepreneurship doesn't follow a nine-to-five schedule. Our businesses have seasons, intense periods of growth, product launches, or client acquisitions followed by relative calm. Trying to maintain perfect equilibrium during these fluctuations is like trying to balance on a seesaw during an earthquake.

The very traits that make us successful entrepreneurs, passion, dedication, and drive, also make traditional balance almost impossible. When you deeply care about your business, the line between work and life naturally blurs.

Shifting the Focus to Work-Life Harmony

The breakthrough came when I stopped pursuing balance and started seeking harmony instead. What's the difference? Balance suggests equal weight, a perfect division. Harmony recognizes that different elements can complement each other even when they're not equal.

Work-life harmony acknowledges that sometimes your business needs more attention, while other times your personal life takes priority. The key is ensuring that these areas work together rather than against each other.

In practice, harmony means:

- Integrating elements of work and life rather than rigidly separating them.
- Allowing your business to flex around core personal commitments.
- Recognizing that fulfillment, not equal time distribution, is the ultimate goal.
- Creating synergy between your business passion and personal well-being.

At KelliWorks, we have embraced this approach by designing our business rhythm around life's natural cycles. We plan our heaviest client workloads outside of school holidays. I schedule deep strategy work during my peak energy hours. We build buffer time into project timelines, acknowledging that life happens.

The result isn't perfect balance; some weeks I still work more than I would like. But there is a profound difference. Instead of feeling perpetually inadequate on both fronts, I experience a sense of wholeness. My business and personal life support rather than sabotage each other. That's the promise of work-life harmony, not a perfectly balanced scale, but a well-played symphony where each element contributes to a beautiful whole.

Setting Boundaries That Stick

The real turning point wasn't some glamorous revelation. It happened on a random Tuesday, on my way to church. I was planning to go to service, as I always did, to pray for "breakthroughs" and "blessings." But that day, a client called, furious about unfinished work that should have been handled. And it clicked: God already blessed me with the business. I didn't need to pray for more favor. I needed to honor the favor I already had.

I realized I was about to **leave my responsibilities** undone to go *look holy* instead of *be accountable.* That shift in thinking changed everything. I stopped asking for miracles and started asking for discipline. I stopped asking for breakthroughs and started *becoming* the breakthrough. I looked in the mirror, really looked, and told myself the truth: "You aren't starving. You aren't without opportunity. You're ordering Uber Eats and feeding the very outcomes you say you want to leave behind." Facing myself was brutal. But it was also beautiful.

Identifying Non-Negotiables in Your Personal and Professional Life

Boundaries aren't just nice-to-have guidelines; they're essential protections for what matters most. I learned this lesson the hard way after missing my son's school play while handling a client "emergency" that, in retrospect, could have waited.

Start by identifying your true non-negotiables. These aren't just preferences but core commitments that, when honored, make everything else possible. Your list might include:

- Essential family commitments (school events, dinner times, weekends)
- Health-preserving routines (sleep, exercise, meditation)
- Dedicated creative or strategic work periods
- Complete disconnection times (vacations, sabbaticals)

The key is being ruthlessly honest about what truly matters. At KelliWorks, we use the "hospital test," if you wouldn't miss it for a hospital visit (barring actual emergencies), it's a non-negotiable.

Keep your list focused; having too many "non-negotiables" means none of them actually are. I maintain just five core boundaries, including never missing my children's performances and preserving weekends for family. Everything else has some flexibility.

Communicating Boundaries Effectively With Your Team and Clients

Having boundaries means nothing if you don't communicate and enforce them. The most common boundary failure isn't external pressure; it's our own reluctance to clearly establish and maintain them.

With your team, be explicit about:

- Your availability hours (when they can expect responses).
- Decision-making protocols during your absence.
- What constitutes a genuine emergency worthy of interruption.
- How you model boundaries (and expect them to have their own).

With clients, set expectations from day one:

- Include your communication policies in onboarding materials.
- Build buffer time into project timelines.
- Train clients on your service model through consistent reinforcement.
- Focus on outcome quality rather than 24/7 availability.

The language you use matters tremendously. Replace apologetic phrasing ("I'm sorry I can't be available") with confident statements ("Our team is available during these hours, which ensures you receive our best work").

Boundaries require maintenance. When a boundary is tested, as it inevitably will be, how you respond sets the precedent. One client continued texting me after hours despite clear policies. Rather than giving in, I waited until business hours to respond and then reiterated our communication protocol. After consistent reinforcement, they adapted.

Prioritizing Self-Care

I realized that how I felt inside would always show up everywhere else: in my business, in my body, and in my bank account. It wasn't about money; it was about integrity, *with myself*.

Today, I live differently:

- I have built healthy habits that nourish me.
- I move through my life (and business) with greater discipline, honesty, and joy.
- I'm becoming the woman of my dreams, not the woman of my nightmares.

And here's the truth I want every entrepreneur to know: If your business success requires you to starve your soul, it isn't success; it's silent suffering. Walking in truth isn't easy. Facing your ego and pride head-on isn't easy. But on the other side? There's life. There's freedom. There's peace.

The Importance of Physical, Emotional, and Mental Well-Being

Neglecting self-care isn't dedication; it's self-sabotage. Your business can't thrive if you're running on empty. Your physical health, emotional resilience, and mental clarity aren't luxuries; they're essential business assets.

Consider the real business costs of neglecting yourself:

- Diminished cognitive function and decision-making.
- Reduced creativity and problem-solving ability.
- Impaired emotional regulation with clients and team.

- Lower productivity despite longer hours.
- Increased risk of serious health issues.

Research confirms what we intuitively know: Entrepreneurs who prioritize well-being actually outperform their burnout-prone counterparts in sustainable business growth, innovation, and leadership effectiveness.

Simple Practices to Incorporate Self-Care Into a Busy Schedule

Self-care doesn't require spa retreats or two-hour yoga sessions (though those are lovely). The most effective practices are simple, sustainable habits integrated into your existing routine:

- **Morning Protection Ritual:** Guard the first 30 minutes of your day for yourself, not your inbox. I use this time for brief meditation, reviewing my priorities, and setting intentions. This small change dramatically impacts my effectiveness and focus.
- **Movement Microbreaks:** Schedule 5-minute movement breaks between meetings. Simple stretching, a brief walk, or quick breathing exercises can reset your nervous system and refresh your mind.
- **Energy-Based Scheduling:** Plan your day according to your natural energy patterns. I schedule

creative and strategic work during my high-energy morning hours, reserving administrative tasks for the afternoons when my focus naturally dips.

- **Digital Boundaries:** Create technology-free zones and times. My non-negotiables include no devices at meals and no email after 8 PM. These small boundaries preserve essential recovery time.
- **Strategic Saying No:** Every "yes" to a nonessential demand is a "no" to your well-being. I've developed a simple filter question: "Will this commitment support my highest priorities or deplete my capacity to fulfill them?"
- **Weekly Recovery Planning:** Just as you plan work meetings, schedule specific recovery time. My calendar includes dedicated blocks for exercise, family time, and complete disconnection-and these appointments are as non-negotiable as client meetings.

Integrating Family and Business

Strategies for Balancing Family Responsibilities With Business Demands

The myth of a perfect separation between family and business life creates unnecessary guilt and struggle. Instead of trying to keep these worlds apart, I have found power in thoughtful integration.

Start by rejecting the false choice between being a good parent and a successful entrepreneur. The most sustainable approach embraces both identities while acknowledging their unique demands. These practical strategies have made a difference for me and many of my clients:

- **Create visible calendars that merge family and business commitments.** My family uses a shared digital calendar that includes both business milestones and family events. This visibility helps everyone understand the full landscape of commitments and prevents scheduling conflicts.
- **Develop clear signals for transitions.** I change my clothes when shifting from work to family mode, creating a physical ritual that helps me mentally transition. Find your own transition ritual, whether it's a brief walk, a specific playlist, or simply closing your laptop with intention.
- **Involve children in your business journey at an age-appropriate level.** My kids understand basic concepts about my business and sometimes visit the office. This demystifies my work and helps them feel connected rather than in competition with it.
- **Build a support network that understands both worlds.** Connect with other entrepreneurial

parents who genuinely understand your challenges. These relationships provide both practical support and emotional validation that generic networking groups often miss.

Time Management for Harmony

Tools and Techniques for Managing Time Effectively

Time management for entrepreneurs isn't about squeezing more tasks into each day. It's about ensuring your finite hours align with what truly matters. After years of hopping between productivity apps and tweaking schedules, I've found these approaches to be the most effective:

- **Time blocking over to-do lists.** Traditional to-do lists create the illusion of productivity without protecting the time needed for execution. Instead, directly schedule blocks of time for specific activities. At KelliWorks, we use three distinct block types: deep work (strategy, creative thinking), shallow work (email, routine tasks), and recovery (breaks, exercise).
- **Energy management alongside time management.** Track your natural energy patterns for two weeks, noting when you feel most focused, creative, or fatigued. Then, align your most demanding

tasks with high-energy periods. I reserve mornings for strategic work because that is when my thinking is clearest.

- **The 2-2-2 Method for maintaining perspective.** Each week, I identify what matters in different timeframes: two days (immediate priorities), two months (mid-range projects), and two years (long-term vision). This prevents urgent tasks from completely overriding important ones.
- **Technology boundaries that serve you.** Use technology intentionally rather than reactively. I batch process emails three times daily, use app blockers during focus periods, and leverage automation and AI-supported technology for routine tasks. The right tech tools should free your attention, not fragment it.

Overcoming Guilt and Fear

Letting Go of the Guilt of Taking Time for Yourself

Entrepreneurial guilt is a silent epidemic. We feel guilty when working (I should be with family), guilty when with family (I should be working), and especially guilty when taking time for ourselves (how can I justify this?). I vividly remember hiding in my car for 20 minutes between appointments, desperately needing rest but feeling ashamed for "wasting time." This guilt doesn't just feel terrible; it's actively harmful to both your business and well-being.

The breakthrough comes from recognizing a fundamental truth: self-care isn't selfish; it's necessary. Think of yourself as a crucial business asset. Would you run your equipment until it breaks? Would you never maintain your technology? Of course not. Yet, we often treat ourselves with less care than we do our laptops.

Start reframing self-care as a strategic investment. My morning workout isn't stealing time from my business. It's enhancing my decision-making, creativity, and leadership capacity. That mental shift transforms guilt into purpose.

Practice these guilt-dissolving approaches:

- Schedule self-care with the same commitment as client meetings.
- Replace "I don't have time for this" with "This isn't a priority" to clarify what you're choosing.
- Keep visible evidence of how self-care improves your performance and presence.

Addressing the Fear of Missing Opportunities or Letting Others Down

Behind much of our boundary-breaking behavior lies fear. Fear of missed opportunities, disappointed clients, or damaged relationships. At its core is the belief that our constant availability is what creates our value.

I spent years saying yes to every client request, convinced that accessibility was my competitive advantage. What I discovered instead was that my perpetual availability diminished my perceived value while increasing my stress.

The counterintuitive truth is that appropriate boundaries enhance rather than damage your professional relationships. When you honor your limits:

- Clients respect your time more, not less.
- Your "yes" carries genuine weight and commitment.
- Your work quality improves, building a stronger reputation.
- You model healthy boundaries for your team and industry.

When the fear of missing out arises, ask yourself, "What am I truly afraid will happen?" Often, the catastrophic consequences we imagine ("I'll lose the client") are dramatically overblown compared to reality ("They'll wait until tomorrow for a response").

Remember that saying no to opportunities that don't align with your priorities creates space for those that do. Every fear-based "yes" to something misaligned is an implicit "no" to something that matters more.

The most transformative question I've learned to ask when feeling guilty or fearful about boundaries is, "What example am I setting for others?" When I maintain healthy limits, I don't just preserve my well-being; I create permission for my team, family, and even clients to do the same.

Steps to Create Sustainable Harmony

Practical Tips for Aligning Business Goals with Personal Values

Sustainable harmony begins when your business objectives and personal values work together rather than against each other. This alignment doesn't happen by accident; it requires intentional design.

Start with a values-based business filter. Identify your core personal values (mine include family connection, growth, and well-being), and then evaluate business decisions through this lens. When considering a new service offering or client relationship, I explicitly ask, "Does this align with my values, or does it compromise them?"

Create boundaries that protect your personal priorities while advancing business goals. For instance, my "no client meetings on Wednesdays" policy initially seemed risky, but it creates space for strategic thinking that ultimately serves clients better while preserving family time.

Redesign your success metrics to include both business and personal indicators. At KelliWorks, our quarterly reviews track not just revenue and client growth but also team well-being, owner satisfaction, and alignment with core values. What gets measured gets managed.

Integrate personal fulfillment into your business model. The most sustainable businesses reflect their owners' authentic strengths and interests. I restructured our service offerings to emphasize advisory work that I genuinely enjoy while delegating technical tasks that drained my energy.

Building Long-Term Habits for Lasting Balance

True harmony isn't achieved through one-time decisions but through consistent habits that gradually reshape your relationship with work and life.

Begin with small, consistent actions rather than dramatic overhauls. Adding a 20-minute morning routine is more sustainable than a complete schedule redesign. These micro-habits create a foundation for larger changes as they become automatic.

Implement regular rhythms and review practices. We conduct monthly "harmony audits" to check the alignment between stated priorities and actual time allocation. This simple practice catches drift before it becomes disconnection.

Build environmental triggers that support your intentions. My laptop closes automatically at 6 PM, and my phone goes into Do Not Disturb mode. These environmental cues make boundaries effortless to maintain.

Practice recovery as systematically as you practice productivity. Schedule complete disconnection periods, whether they are screen-free evenings, device-free weekends, or actual vacations. These recovery periods aren't indulgences; they're essential for sustainable performance. Remember that harmony isn't a destination but a continuous practice. Some weeks will flow smoothly, while others will feel chaotic. The goal isn't perfection but the resilience to return to your intentions when life inevitably pulls you off course.

By consistently aligning your business decisions with your personal values and building sustainable habits, you create something more valuable than mere success. You create a life and business that truly work together.

CHAPTER 6

THE DELEGATION REVOLUTION

You've built the systems. You've assembled the team. You've created the processes. Yet somehow, you're still working 60-hour weeks and handling tasks that don't reflect your unique value. If this sounds familiar, you've hit the final barrier to true business freedom: the delegation challenge.

Effective delegation isn't just about offloading tasks; it's about fundamentally reimagining your role as a business owner. It's the difference between being buried in day-to-day operations and leading a business that serves your life rather than consuming it.

In this chapter, we'll explore how to master the art of letting go, transforming both your business capacity and your quality of life in the process.

Why Letting Go Is Essential for Growth

I remember the moment I realized I had become the biggest obstacle to my own business growth. We had just lost a major client opportunity because I couldn't personally handle the additional workload, despite having a capable team standing by. My need to control every aspect of the business wasn't just exhausting me; it was actively limiting our potential.

The hard truth for every entrepreneur is that you cannot grow beyond your personal capacity unless you master delegation. Your time, energy, and attention are finite resources. When you insist on being involved in every aspect of your business, you create a ceiling, not just for your company's growth, but for your own freedom and fulfillment.

Effective delegation isn't just about managing workload; it's about multiplication. When you properly transfer tasks and authority, you expand your business's capabilities exponentially. Tasks that once consumed your day can happen simultaneously across your team, creating growth that would be impossible through your efforts alone.

Overcoming the "I Have to Do It All" Mentality

The "I have to do it all" mentality typically stems from three core beliefs:

- **The Perfectionist Trap:** "Nobody can do it as well as I can."
- **The Irreplaceability Myth:** "My personal involvement is what clients expect."
- **The Speed Illusion:** "It's faster to do it myself than to teach someone else."

I held all these beliefs fiercely. Each seemed rational, even responsible. However, examining them honestly revealed their flaws.

The perfectionist trap ignores the fact that "different" doesn't mean "worse," and sometimes, team members bring perspectives that improve upon your approach. The irreplaceability myth confuses your value with your tasks; clients value outcomes, not your personal handling of every detail. Additionally, the speed illusion focuses on short-term efficiency while ignoring long-term capacity.

Breaking free starts with a mindset shift: Delegation isn't about abdicating responsibility but rather multiplying capability. It's about recognizing that your highest value lies not in doing everything but in enabling others to succeed.

Begin by questioning each instance of "I have to do this myself" with "Is this truly the best use of my unique abilities?" At KelliWorks, this single question helped me identify dozens of tasks I was handling out of habit rather than necessity.

The Benefits of Delegation

Freeing Up Your Time for Strategic Leadership

When I first started tracking my time, I discovered something alarming. I was spending over 70% of my day on tasks that did not utilize my unique skills or drive business growth. Client follow-ups, basic bookkeeping, and routine problem-solving consumed hours that should have been dedicated to strategic thinking and business development.

Effective delegation creates space for what only you can do. At KelliWorks, my first serious delegation effort freed up 15 hours weekly, time I redirected to developing new service offerings that increased our revenue by 32% within six months. This isn't just about working less; it's about focusing your limited time on high-leverage activities that truly move the needle.

Strategic leadership requires mental space and energy that are consumed by operational details. When you're constantly switching between client emails, team questions, and administrative tasks, you cannot access the deep thinking needed for innovation and growth. Delegation creates the cognitive bandwidth for strategic work.

Consider this: What could you accomplish with 10 more hours each week dedicated solely to your highest-value contributions? What opportunities are you missing because you are buried in tasks that others could handle?

Empowering Your Team to Take Ownership

Perhaps the most overlooked benefit of delegation is its impact on your team. When handled properly, delegation is not just task transfer; it is capability building.

Team members who receive meaningful responsibility with appropriate support develop faster than those who simply execute instructions. When I delegated client onboarding to Sarah, she did not just follow my process; she improved it, reducing our setup time by 40% while increasing client satisfaction scores.

Ownership creates engagement. Research consistently shows that autonomy and mastery are primary motivators for knowledge workers. When team members can make decisions, solve problems, and see their impact, their commitment deepens. At KelliWorks, our engagement scores increased by 27% after implementing structured delegation practices.

By holding onto tasks that others could handle, you are not just limiting your time; you are limiting your team's growth. Every task you refuse to delegate is a learning opportunity denied, a chance for someone to develop skills and confidence.

What to Delegate and What to Keep

Identifying Tasks That Can Be Delegated

Not all tasks are created equal when it comes to delegation potential. The key is to develop a systematic approach to identifying what you should transfer to others.

Start with the "Delegation Matrix" we use at KelliWorks. Evaluate each of your current activities against these criteria:

- **Repetitive nature:** Tasks that follow consistent patterns are prime candidates for delegation.
- **Skill alignment:** Activities that do not require your unique expertise.
- **Growth potential:** Tasks that could help develop team members' capabilities.
- **Time consumption:** Low-value activities that consume a disproportionate amount of time.

The most effective delegation targets typically include:

- Administrative tasks (scheduling, data entry, basic correspondence)

- Technical processes with clear parameters (bookkeeping, report generation)
- Routine client interactions (onboarding, regular updates, standard questions)
- Research and information gathering (market research, competitor analysis)
- Basic problem-solving within established frameworks

Be especially vigilant about tasks you are holding onto because "it's easier to do it myself." These are often the ones creating the biggest bottlenecks in your business. At KelliWorks, I discovered that I was spending five hours weekly personally handling client report generation, work that was perfectly suited for delegation once it was properly documented.

Understanding High-Value Activities That Require Your Focus

Just as important as knowing what to delegate is understanding what deserves your personal attention. Your highest-value activities typically fall into the following categories:

- **Strategic Direction:** Vision-setting, long-term planning, and major pivots. Only you can determine where your business should be heading and why.

- **Key Relationships:** Certain client and partner relationships benefit from owner involvement, particularly in their establishment and maintenance of trust.
- **Essential Decision-Making:** While many decisions can and should be delegated, some fundamental choices about business direction, significant investments, or core values require your judgment.
- **Unique Expertise:** Activities that leverage your specific knowledge, skills, or reputation that genuinely cannot be replicated by others.
- **Culture Leadership:** Modeling and reinforcing your business values and expectations, the "how we do things here" that shapes your team environment.

The litmus test I apply is, "Is this something only I can do, or something I'm uniquely positioned to do best?" If the answer is no, it is a candidate for delegation.

Remember that "what to keep" evolves as your business grows. Activities that demanded your attention in the early stages may become perfect delegation opportunities as your team develops and your strategic priorities shift.

Building Trust and Accountability

Creating Clear Expectations and Providing Support

Delegation failures rarely stem from team members' incompetence; they usually result from unclear expectations. I learned this lesson the hard way after delegating client reporting, only to receive work that missed the mark entirely. The problem wasn't my team member's abilities; it was my vague instructions and assumptions. Effective delegation requires crystal-clear expectations across multiple dimensions:

- **Outcome clarity:** Define what success looks like in specific, measurable terms. Instead of saying "create a client report," specify "produce a financial summary showing monthly cash flow, aging receivables, and year-to-date profit margin comparisons."
- **Authority boundaries:** Clearly outline decision-making parameters. We use a simple framework: decisions the person can make independently, decisions requiring consultation, and decisions needing approval.
- **Timeline and milestones:** Establish not just final deadlines but also check-in points to prevent last-minute surprises. For major responsibilities, we set 25%, 50%, and 75% completion check-ins.

- **Quality standards:** Communicate the level of polish expected and any non-negotiable requirements. Is this client-ready work or an internal draft? Are there compliance considerations or brand standards to maintain?

Fostering a Culture of Ownership and Responsibility

Trust and accountability flourish in an environment where ownership is valued and supported. Build this culture through deliberate practices:

- **Delegate outcomes, not just tasks:** Focus on the "what" and "why" rather than dictating the "how." This creates space for initiative and innovation rather than mere compliance.
- **Implement appropriate check-ins:** Balance oversight with autonomy. Too many check-ins signal distrust, while too few can leave team members feeling unsupported. Find the middle ground that provides safety without micromanagement.
- **Create clarity around consequences:** Ensure everyone understands both the positive outcomes of success and the implications of missed expectations. This isn't about punishment but about transparent cause-and-effect relationships.
- **Celebrate examples of ownership:** Publicly recognize team members who take initiative, solve

problems independently, or go beyond basic compliance. What gets recognized gets repeated.

- **Address accountability gaps promptly:** When expectations aren't met, address the situation directly but constructively. Focus on learning and improvement rather than assigning blame.

The ultimate test of your delegation culture isn't whether tasks get completed; it's whether your team feels personally invested in the outcomes. When team members start saying "my client" instead of "your client" or "our process" instead of "the company's process," you'll know you've created true ownership.

Systems for Effective Delegation

Using Tools to Assign and Track Tasks Efficiently

Effective delegation requires more than good intentions; it needs systematic support. At KelliWorks, we discovered that without proper tracking systems, delegated tasks often fell through the cracks or required constant follow-up, which negated the time savings.

The right tools create accountability without micromanagement:

- **Centralized task management platforms** keep delegated responsibilities visible to everyone involved. We use a project management system that allows us to assign tasks, set deadlines, establish priorities, and track progress in real time. This transparency eliminates the need for constant status updates while ensuring that nothing gets overlooked.

- **Responsibility matrices** clarify ownership across recurring business functions. Our RACI charts (Responsible, Accountable, Consulted, Informed) define who handles each aspect of key processes, eliminating confusion about who should be doing what.
- **Automated reminders and notifications** remove the burden of manual follow-up. Our system sends automatic alerts for approaching deadlines and overdue tasks, helping team members manage their workload without constant prompting.
- **Regular review mechanisms** ensure that delegated responsibilities stay on track. We conduct brief weekly reviews of all delegated projects, addressing potential bottlenecks before they become problems.

The key is selecting tools that support your workflow rather than forcing your team to adapt to complicated systems. We initially implemented an overly complex project management platform that created more work than it saved. The best delegation tools are intuitive enough that team members actually use them consistently.

Documenting Processes for Seamless Handoffs

Even the most talented team members cannot succeed with delegation if they do not understand how to perform the tasks. Process documentation is the bridge that transfers knowledge efficiently:

- **Visual process maps** provide step-by-step guidance that is easy to follow. We create flowcharts for complex processes, highlighting decision points and alternative paths. These visual guides are far more effective than text-heavy manuals.
- **Video tutorials** capture nuances that written instructions might miss. For client-facing tasks like onboarding calls, we record videos demonstrating not just what to do but also how to do it with the right tone and emphasis.
- **Checklists and templates** reduce cognitive load and ensure consistency. Our team has standardised templates for everything from client emails to meeting agendas, making delegation smoother while maintaining quality standards.
- **Decision guidelines** empower independent action within boundaries. Instead of rigid procedures, we provide frameworks that help team members make sound decisions when facing variables or exceptions.

The most effective documentation anticipates questions and provides context, not just commands. We have learned to include the "why" behind processes, helping team members understand the purpose and importance of tasks rather than just mechanically following steps.

Overcoming Common Delegation Challenges

Addressing Resistance to Letting Go

Even when you intellectually understand the importance of delegation, emotional resistance can still sabotage your efforts. I have worked with hundreds of business owners, and the same patterns of resistance appear consistently:

- **The perfectionist trap:** "They won't do it exactly my way." This mindset confuses "different" with "wrong." The breakthrough comes when you realize that sometimes team members' methods may actually be better than yours, and even when they are just different, the value of freeing your time often outweighs minor variations in approach.
- **The identity crisis:** "If I'm not doing everything, what's my value?" Many entrepreneurs tie their worth to their daily tasks rather than to their vision and leadership. Redefining your contribution as

building capacity rather than completing tasks creates space for letting go.

- **The speed misconception:** "It's faster to do it myself." While this may be true for a single instance, it ignores the cumulative cost of repeatedly handling tasks that could be systematized and delegated. Apply the "10x rule": If you will do this task more than ten times, the time investment in delegation pays off.
- **The control illusion:** "I need to maintain control over everything." The irony is that being buried in tactical work actually reduces your control over strategic outcomes. True control comes from building systems and teams that reliably deliver results, not from personally handling every detail.

The most effective strategy for overcoming resistance is gradual delegation. Start with lower-risk tasks, build confidence in the process, and progressively expand your delegation comfort zone as you experience the benefits firsthand.

Navigating Mistakes and Miscommunications

Delegation inevitably involves some missteps, especially in the beginning. How you handle these challenges determines whether delegation becomes sustainable or remains a source of frustration:

- **Adopt a learning orientation** toward mistakes. When a delegated task doesn't meet expectations, approach it as a systems problem rather than a people problem. Ask, "What was missing from our process that would have prevented this mistake?"
- **Create safe feedback loops** that encourage honest communication. We implement "early warning" protocols where team members can flag potential issues without fear of judgment. This prevents small misunderstandings from becoming major problems.
- **Implement the rule of "fix, then analyze."** When mistakes happen, first address the immediate situation, then step back to examine the root cause. This prevents emotional reactions while ensuring systemic improvement.
- **Use miscommunications as documentation opportunities.** Each misunderstanding reveals a gap in your delegation system. When a team member misinterprets instructions, it highlights where your process documentation needs clarification.

Steps to Start Delegating Today

Identifying Your First Delegation Opportunities

The journey toward effective delegation doesn't require a complete business overhaul. Start with strategic, manageable steps that build confidence and momentum:

Begin with a time audit. Track your activities for one week, categorizing each task by importance, complexity, and whether it requires your unique skills. Look for patterns of low-value work that consume significant time. At KelliWorks, I discovered that I was spending seven hours weekly on basic client correspondence that could easily be templated and delegated.

Apply the "Delegation Decision Matrix." Evaluate tasks against these criteria:

- Is it repetitive?
- Does it require your unique expertise?
- Could someone else do it 80% as well?
- Would delegating it create growth opportunities for your team?

Tasks that are repetitive, do not require your unique skills, could be done adequately by others, and provide development opportunities are your perfect first delegation candidates.

Start with "low-risk, high-time" tasks. Look for responsibilities that consume significant time but where mistakes would not be catastrophic. Email management, basic research, standard client follow-ups, and routine reporting often fall into this category.

Identify your energy drains. Some tasks might not take much time but deplete your energy disproportionately. These emotional drains are often excellent candidates for delegation, freeing not just your schedule but also your mental bandwidth.

Gradually Building a Delegation Framework for Your Business

With your initial delegation targets identified, implement a systematic approach to transfer responsibilities effectively:

Create a three-phase delegation plan for each responsibility:

1. **Shadow Phase:** The team member observes you completing the task while you document the process.
2. **Reverse Shadow Phase:** They perform the task while you observe and provide feedback.
3. **Independence Phase:** They handle the responsibility independently with scheduled check-ins.

Document as you delegate. Rather than trying to create perfect documentation before delegating, build your processes during the transition. Have the team member document their understanding of the task as they learn it, creating resources that will streamline future delegation.

Establish success metrics for delegated responsibilities. Clear, measurable outcomes create confidence for both you and your team. For client follow-up emails, metrics might include response time, resolution rate, and client satisfaction scores.

Implement graduated authority levels as confidence builds. Start by requiring approvals for decisions, then move to notifications only, and finally to periodic reviews of independently handled work.

Create a delegation pipeline that constantly identifies new opportunities. Schedule quarterly reviews to identify additional tasks you can transfer as your team develops capabilities and your business needs evolve.

Remember that effective delegation is a skill developed through practice. Each successful handoff builds your confidence and your team's capabilities. Start small, celebrate wins, learn from challenges, and gradually expand your delegation comfort zone.

The most powerful question to ask yourself each week is, "What am I doing now that I shouldn't be doing six months from now?" Let the answer guide your delegation journey toward true business freedom.

CHAPTER 7

GROWTH WITHOUT SACRIFICE

The traditional entrepreneurial narrative glorifies growth at all costs-scaling quickly, working relentlessly, and prioritizing business above everything else. But what if expansion didn't have to mean sacrifice? What if you could grow your business while actually improving your quality of life?

This isn't just a pleasant theory; it's entirely possible with the right approach. The entrepreneurs who successfully scale without burnout aren't superhuman; they've simply mastered the art of building businesses that expand through systems rather than through personal sacrifice.

In this chapter, we'll explore how to create growth that enhances rather than diminishes your life, expansion that works for you, not against you.

Growth Without Sacrifice

The Challenge of Balancing Expansion and Sustainability

The entrepreneurial journey often presents a seemingly impossible choice: grow your business or preserve your sanity. I've watched countless business owners fall into the expansion trap, their revenues increase while their quality of life plummets. Their calendars fill with more meetings, their teams expand with additional management challenges, and their to-do lists grow exponentially longer.

This pattern isn't inevitable; it's the result of a fundamental misconception about growth. Most entrepreneurs approach expansion additively, simply doing more of what they are already doing. More clients mean more work. More revenue means more complexity. More opportunities mean more of your personal time and energy.

The challenge lies in breaking this linear relationship between business growth and personal sacrifice. True sustainability comes from designing systems where revenue and impact can scale without proportionally increasing your workload or stress.

Why Prioritizing Balance Is Crucial During Growth

Balance isn't just a nice-to-have during expansion; it's strategically essential. Consider these critical reasons:

- **Decision quality deteriorates under pressure.** Research consistently shows that cognitive function declines with exhaustion and stress. The strategic decisions required during growth phases demand your best thinking, not your depleted remnants.
- **Growth amplifies existing problems.** Whatever isn't working in your business now will only become more problematic as you scale. Addressing balance and sustainability issues before expansion is like fixing the foundation before adding another floor to your house.
- **Opportunity evaluation requires perspective.** Without balance, every potential opportunity appears necessary. The overwhelmed entrepreneur often can't distinguish between distractions and true strategic openings, leading to scattered efforts rather than focused growth.
- **Culture flows from the top.** If you're burning out during expansion, you're modeling unsustainable patterns for your entire organization. Teams take their cues from leadership, creating a cascading effect of overwork and imbalance.

Entrepreneurs who maintain balance during growth aren't just happier; they're more successful. They make clearer decisions, attract and retain better talent, and build businesses with staying power rather than experiencing flash-in-the-pan growth followed by collapse.

The question isn't whether you can afford to prioritize balance during growth; it's whether you can afford not to.

Scalable Systems for Expansion

Designing Processes That Grow With Your Business

The difference between businesses that falter under expansion and those that thrive is often found in their process architecture. Scalable processes aren't just about handling current demands; they are designed to accommodate growth without requiring proportional increases in resources or oversight.

At KelliWorks, we learned this lesson through trial and error. Our initial client onboarding process worked beautifully for 15 clients but collapsed entirely when we reached 30. The system relied too heavily on my personal touchpoints and lacked clear handoffs between team members.

Truly scalable processes share these characteristics:

- **Modular design** allows components to be upgraded or modified without disrupting the entire system. We restructured our service delivery into distinct modules that could be assigned to different team members as volume increased.

- **Clear decision frameworks** enable team members to handle variations independently. Rather than requiring manager input for every deviation, we created guidelines that empowered staff to make appropriate adjustments within defined parameters.
- **Standardized inputs and outputs** ensure consistency regardless of who executes the process. Each step in our client workflow now has specific requirements for what comes in and goes out, maintaining quality as different people handle different stages.
- **Documented capacity limits** identify when processes need to evolve. We established metrics for each system (clients per manager, transactions per bookkeeper) with trigger points that signal when restructuring is necessary before problems emerge.

When designing processes for scale, resist the temptation to optimize solely for today's needs. Build with tomorrow's growth in mind, even if it seems slightly inefficient for your current size.

Leveraging Automation and Technology for Efficiency

Automation is the secret weapon of sustainable growth. It breaks the linear relationship between business expansion and increased workload. The right technology investments create capacity without requiring proportional increases in time or staffing.

Focus first on automating these high-impact areas:

- **Repetitive communications**, such as appointment reminders, follow-ups, and status updates. Our automated client communication system now handles over 60% of routine touchpoints without human intervention, saving dozens of hours weekly while improving consistency.
- **Data transfer between systems** eliminates double entry and reduces errors. We implemented integrations between our CRM, accounting software, and project management tools, creating a single source of truth that updates automatically across platforms.
- **Document generation and management** for proposals, contracts, and client deliverables. Templates with variable fields now produce customized materials in minutes rather than hours, maintaining our professional standards regardless of volume.
- **Monitoring and alerts** that identify exceptions requiring human attention. Our dashboard highlights unusual patterns or potential issues, allowing for proactive intervention before clients notice problems.

The most successful automation strategies focus on augmenting rather than replacing human capabilities. Technology handles the routine, repetitive aspects of your business, freeing your team to apply their judgment, creativity, and relationship skills where they create the most value.

Remember, automation implemented during periods of stability creates capacity for growth. Waiting until you're already overwhelmed makes implementation itself a burden rather than a relief.

Replicating Success

Standardizing Best Practices Across Multiple Locations or Teams

As KelliWorks expanded from one office to three, we encountered a challenge familiar to growing businesses: the "it worked when it was just us" syndrome. Practices that functioned smoothly with our original team began to break down across multiple locations, creating inconsistent results and operational friction.

The key to successful replication lies in identifying what truly drives your success. Not every practice needs standardization. Focus on your critical differentiators and non-negotiable quality standards. At KelliWorks, we distinguished between:

- **Core Standards:** Elements essential to our brand promise and client experience that must remain consistent everywhere. These include our initial client assessment process, regular communication protocols, and financial reporting frameworks.

- **Local Adaptations:** Areas where teams can customize approaches to address regional needs or leverage specific talents. We allowed flexibility in team meeting structures and community engagement strategies while maintaining outcome consistency.

Effective standardization requires more than documentation; it needs systematic transfer mechanisms:

- **Playbooks and visual guides** that capture not just what to do but also why and how. Our service team playbooks include process maps, decision frameworks, and examples of both successful and problematic cases.
- **Cross-location training and mentoring** that build relationships between teams. We implemented a “sister office” program where experienced team members temporarily work alongside newer locations to transfer tacit knowledge that documentation cannot capture.
- **Regular best practice sharing forums** where innovations from any location can be evaluated for broader implementation. These structured

exchanges prevent silos while allowing improvements to spread organically throughout the organization.

Creating Consistency in Customer Experience and Operations

Client experience consistency becomes increasingly challenging as you scale. Yet, it is often what differentiates thriving businesses from those that plateau or decline during expansion.

Start by mapping your client journey from initial contact through ongoing service delivery, identifying each touchpoint and interaction. For each point, establish:

- **Experience standards** that define what clients should feel and receive. Rather than dictating exact scripts, these standards focus on outcomes such as "clients should feel heard and understood during the intake process," with specific indicators of success.
- **Quality assurance mechanisms** that verify consistent delivery. Our regular client experience surveys measure the same key factors across all locations, allowing us to identify and address variations quickly.
- **Feedback loops** that capture and address inconsistencies. We implemented a simple system where clients can rate each interaction, with ratings below

a certain threshold triggering immediate review and response.

The most powerful tool for maintaining consistency is a strong, well-articulated culture. When team members across locations share the same values and understand what truly matters to your business, they make similar decisions even when facing novel situations.

At KelliWorks, we reinforced our culture during expansion through:

- Regular all-team gatherings focused on our core purpose and values.
- Recognition programs highlighting examples of our principles in action.
- Leadership development that emphasizes cultural stewardship.
- Hiring processes that prioritize value alignment alongside technical skills.

Perfect uniformity is not the goal; rather, it is consistency in the outcomes that matter most to your clients and your business's success. Allow room for personality and local adaptation while maintaining unwavering standards in your true differentiators.

Maintaining Quality During Growth

Strategies for Avoiding Growing Pains That Lead to Burnout

Growth creates natural pressure points that, if left unaddressed, lead to quality deterioration and team burnout. The businesses that maintain excellence during expansion anticipate these challenges rather than react to them. Start by identifying your quality vulnerabilities, the areas most likely to suffer during rapid growth. We recognized that our detailed financial reviews were at risk as client volume increased. Rather than waiting for quality to slip, we proactively redesigned our review process with scalability in mind, creating tiered review protocols based on complexity and risk factors.

Implement these preventive strategies before growth strains your operations:

- **Capacity buffers** that maintain breathing room in your systems. Operating at 100% capacity leaves no margin for unexpected demands or opportunities. We maintain a 20% capacity reserve across all departments, ensuring that teams can absorb growth surges without compromising quality.
- **Graduated service models** that align resource intensity with client needs. Not every client requires your highest-touch service level. Our tiered service

approach ensures appropriate attention based on complexity and requirements, preventing team overextension while maintaining client satisfaction.

- **Strategic pacing** of growth initiatives. Simultaneous expansion across multiple fronts virtually guarantees burnout. When opening our third location, we deliberately slowed new client acquisition in established offices, allowing resources and attention to focus on successful expansion.
- **Preemptive team expansion** rather than reactive hiring. Bringing in new team members after you are already overwhelmed means you lack the capacity to properly train and integrate them. Hire ahead of your growth curve, giving new team members time to fully absorb your culture and processes.

Monitoring Performance and Addressing Issues Early

Even the best preventive strategies require vigilant monitoring. Establish early warning systems that identify potential issues before they impact client experience or team well-being:

- **Leading indicators** that predict future problems rather than merely measuring past performance. While most businesses track revenue and client satisfaction, these metrics lag behind operational issues. We monitor indicators such as average response time, process exceptions, and team capacity utilization, signals that highlight potential quality risks before they affect outcomes.

- **Regular quality audits** conducted by fresh eyes. When teams are busy with growth demands, subtle quality slippage often goes unnoticed. Our cross-team review program includes members from each location who periodically audit work from other offices, applying consistent standards and identifying drift.
- **Anonymous feedback channels** for team members to report concerns. Those closest to the work often notice problems first but may hesitate to raise issues formally. Our anonymous "quality alert" system allows anyone to flag concerns without fear of negative consequences.
- **Systematic issue triage** that distinguishes between isolated incidents and systemic problems. Not every issue requires a complete process overhaul. Our three-category approach classifies problems as one-time anomalies, training opportunities, or system failures, each with appropriate response protocols.

When quality issues do emerge, address them directly and transparently. At KelliWorks, we implement a three-part response to significant quality challenges:

1. Immediate client impact mitigation
2. Root cause analysis
3. Systematic correction and preventive measures

Delegation at Scale

Expanding Your Team and Leadership Structure

As we discussed in the previous chapter, effective delegation is essential for business freedom. However, as your company grows, simple one-to-one delegation evolves into something more complex. The leadership structure that served you well with a small team often buckles under the weight of expansion.

At KelliWorks, we initially tried to maintain our flat structure as we grew from five to fifteen team members. The result? I became the bottleneck for dozens of daily decisions, while team members lacked the guidance and support they needed. Creating an effective leadership layer became essential for sustainable expansion.

Develop your leadership structure incrementally rather than attempting a wholesale reorganization:

- **Identify natural leaders** who already informally guide others. Before creating official management positions, we recognized team members who consistently helped colleagues and maintained quality standards. These informal leaders became our first tier of leadership.
- **Create focused leadership roles** rather than general management positions. Instead of generic "managers," we established specific roles like Client Experience Lead and Technical Standards Director, allowing team members to lead in their areas of strength rather than forcing them into all-purpose management.
- **Build leadership capacity before it is urgently needed.** We implemented a Leadership Development Program that prepares high-potential team members for future roles, creating a pipeline of leaders who understand our culture and systems before taking on formal authority.
- **Clarify decision rights across leadership levels.** As leadership tiers develop, clearly define who makes which decisions. Our Decision Authority

Matrix specifies which matters require owner input, which can be handled by department leaders, and which individual team members can address independently.

Trusting Managers and Leaders to Uphold Your Vision

Many entrepreneurs struggle with the emotional challenge of trusting others to maintain their standards and vision. This challenge intensifies at scale when you entrust your brand to leaders who may make different decisions than you would.

Build trust through a systematic approach rather than blind faith:

- **Articulate your non-negotiables** with crystal clarity. Before delegating authority to leaders, define the principles and standards that are not open to interpretation. Our Leadership Constitution outlines core values and fundamental approaches that define how we operate, regardless of who is making decisions.
- **Create alignment through involvement rather than dictation.** Leaders who participate in developing strategies and standards feel ownership rather than mere compliance. When establishing our growth plan, we involved all department heads

in creating the roadmap, ensuring their genuine buy-in rather than superficial agreement.

- **Implement appropriate oversight mechanisms** that provide visibility without micromanagement. Our leadership dashboard displays key performance indicators for each department, allowing me to monitor outcomes without getting involved in the details of daily execution.
- **Allow controlled failure as a learning tool.** Leaders develop judgment through experience, including mistakes. Create safe spaces for leaders to make recoverable errors that build their capabilities without endangering client relationships or business stability.

The ultimate trust exercise is not hands-off abdication but rather purposeful empowerment. At KelliWorks, we define success not as leaders making the same decisions I would make, but as making decisions that honor our core values and deliver excellent results, even when their approach differs from mine.

Aligning Growth With Personal Well-Being

Reassessing Priorities as Your Business Expands

Growth inevitably changes your business, but it should enhance rather than diminish your life. As your company expands, regular reassessment of priorities becomes essential to maintain alignment between business growth and personal fulfillment.

Many entrepreneurs fall into the trap of allowing expansion to dictate their evolving roles without conscious choice. During the opening of our second location, I found myself pulled back into operational details that I had successfully delegated years earlier. Suddenly, I was working longer hours on tasks that did not leverage my strengths or bring me satisfaction.

Create a deliberate process for reassessing your role as growth occurs:

- **Schedule quarterly personal strategy sessions** to evaluate how your time aligns with your priorities. During these reflections, I review where my hours are going and whether these activities reflect my highest contributions to the business and my personal fulfillment.
- **Revisit your definition of success** as your business reaches new levels. The metrics that mattered in the early stages (revenue growth, client acquisition) may need to evolve toward different indicators (profit margin, team development, community impact) that better reflect your current priorities.

- **Re-examine your unique abilities** in the context of your expanding organization. As we grew, I realized my greatest value had shifted from technical expertise to vision setting and culture development, areas I needed to prioritize rather than being pulled back into operational details.
- **Consider the personal impact** of each growth opportunity before pursuing it. I now evaluate potential expansions not just for financial returns but also for their effects on work complexity, team culture, and my personal engagement. Some "good business opportunities" are not good life opportunities.

Setting Boundaries to Protect Your Time and Energy

As your business grows, setting boundaries becomes more challenging and crucial. The demands multiply, the stakes increase, and the pressure to be available intensifies. Without deliberate protection, your time and energy quickly become casualties of expansion.

Implement these boundary-protecting practices:

- **Create structural buffers** that protect your priorities. I have established "Focus Days" every Wednesday when I am completely unavailable for routine matters. These days are dedicated to strategic work, relationship building, and personal renewal, the activities that most directly support sustainable growth.

- **Develop escalation protocols** that filter what reaches you. As we discussed in the delegation chapter, not every decision requires your input. Our three-tier escalation framework ensures that only truly significant issues reach my attention, preventing the "leadership as bottleneck" syndrome that is common in growing businesses.
- **Establish technology boundaries** that prevent constant interruption. Growth often brings more communication channels and more frequent notifications. I follow a "notification hierarchy" where only urgent matters trigger immediate alerts, while other communications wait for designated review times.
- **Maintain physical and mental renewal practices** that scale with business demands. As pressure increases, many entrepreneurs sacrifice the very practices that enable them to handle growth effectively. I schedule physical activity, reflection time, and completely unplugged weekends as nonnegotiable commitments that actually increase as business demands intensify.

The ultimate boundary as your business grows is the boundary of identity, separating who you are from what your business achieves. When your sense of self becomes too entangled with business outcomes, expansion becomes personally threatening rather than fulfilling.

Creating a Sustainable Vision for the Future

Defining What Success Looks Like Beyond Financial Metrics

The entrepreneurial journey often begins with straightforward financial goals: survival, stability, and eventually, prosperity. However, as those initial milestones are achieved, many business owners experience a surprising emptiness. The question shifts from "How can I make this work?" to "Why am I doing this at all?"

I hit this wall after reaching what I had once considered the pinnacle of success. Revenue targets were exceeded, the team was growing, and everything looked impressive on paper. Yet, I felt strangely disconnected from the business I had built. Something was missing.

The breakthrough came when I expanded my definition of success beyond financial metrics. True success is multidimensional, encompassing:

- **Purpose fulfillment:** How well does your business allow you to express your deeper "why"? I realized my greatest satisfaction came not from managing financials but from seeing clients transform their relationships with their businesses.

- **Personal growth:** Does your business challenge you to become your best self? Growth that demands your evolution rather than just your effort creates lasting fulfillment.
- **Relationship quality:** How do your business activities impact your most important relationships? Success that comes at the cost of connection with loved ones is ultimately hollow.
- **Health and vitality:** Does your business enhance or diminish your physical and mental well-being? Sustainable success energizes rather than depletes you.
- **Community impact:** What positive difference does your business make beyond profit? I found deep meaning in creating employment opportunities and supporting our local community.

Creating metrics for these dimensions was transformative. When quarterly reviews included not just financial results but also team development, client transformation stories, personal growth milestones, and community contributions, my engagement soared.

Building a Legacy That Reflects Your Values and Goals

Legacy thinking shifts your perspective from immediate results to lasting impact. It asks not what your business is achieving today, but what it will have contributed when you are no longer at the helm.

Start by clarifying your core values, not generic business platitudes, but the genuine principles that guide your life. My values of authenticity, growth, and service became the foundation for legacy decisions that sometimes contradicted conventional business wisdom.

A legacy-oriented business makes choices based on long-term impact rather than short-term gain:

- **Investing in people development,** even when the ROI is not immediately measurable. The leaders I have helped develop will continue to create a positive impact long after my direct involvement ends.
- **Building sustainable systems** rather than depending on heroic effort. A business that requires constant intervention is not a legacy; it is a burden.
- **Creating a culture that perpetuates your values** without requiring your presence. When team members naturally make decisions aligned with your principles, your impact extends far beyond your tenure.
- **Considering succession planning early**, not as an exit strategy but as a stewardship responsibility.

> I began developing potential future leaders years before I considered stepping back from daily operations.

Your business should be one of your life's great expressions, not its greatest regret. When built thoughtfully, it becomes a vehicle for creating lasting impact while enhancing your life in the present-the ultimate sustainable vision.

CHAPTER 8

THE LEADERSHIP EVOLUTION

The most profound business transformation isn't about systems, processes, or even team structure. It's about how you evolve as a leader. Many entrepreneurs start as competent technicians, become skilled managers, but struggle to grow into visionary leaders capable of inspiring others.

I have walked this path myself, transitioning from a hands-on controller of every detail to someone who empowers others to exceed what I could accomplish alone. This evolution didn't happen by accident, and it certainly wasn't easy. It required confronting deeply held beliefs about control, trust, and my own identity as a business owner.

In this chapter, we will explore the leadership journey that unlocks your business's true potential.

The Leadership Evolution

From Task Manager to Visionary Leader

My leadership journey began like that of most entrepreneurs, deeply embedded in daily operations, personally handling client work, and directing every aspect of the business. I measured my value by tasks completed and fires extinguished. This hands-on approach served me well in the startup phase but eventually became the very thing that limited our growth.

The evolution from task manager to visionary leader occurs in stages, each requiring a different mindset and skill set:

- **The Technician Phase:** Here, you are primarily focused on delivering your core service or product. Your success comes from technical expertise and personal productivity. I spent my early years perfecting client deliverables and handling every financial review personally.
- **The Manager Phase:** As your business grows, you begin coordinating others rather than doing everything yourself. Success now depends on your ability to organize, delegate, and monitor performance. I found myself creating systems, assigning tasks, and ensuring that quality standards were met.

- **The Leader Phase:** The true breakthrough comes when you shift from managing processes to inspiring people. Leadership is about setting direction, cultivating culture, and developing others. This requires you to articulate a compelling vision, nurture team capabilities, and focus on where you are going rather than just what you are doing.

This evolution is not just about changing what you do; it is about transforming who you are in relation to your business. The hardest part for me was not learning new skills but letting go of the identity I had built as the person who "makes things happen."

Why Leadership Style Impacts Business Growth

Your leadership style creates either a ceiling or a launching pad for your business potential. I have witnessed this reality both in my own company and with hundreds of clients:

- **Directive leadership** (telling people exactly what to do and how to do it) creates efficiency in the short term but limits scalability. When every decision flows through you, growth inevitably stalls at the limits of your personal capacity.
- **Delegative leadership** moves beyond directing tasks to assigning outcomes, creating space for

team members to develop solutions. This approach multiplies your impact but requires clear expectations and appropriate support.

- **Transformational leadership** focuses on inspiring purpose, developing capabilities, and fostering innovation. This style creates organizations capable of evolving and thriving far beyond what any individual could design or control.

The impact of leadership style extends beyond operational capacity to affect every aspect of business performance:

- **Team engagement** rises dramatically when people feel inspired rather than merely directed. I observed our retention rate double after shifting from directive to transformational leadership, with corresponding improvements in productivity and initiative.
- **Innovation capacity** expands when leadership creates psychological safety for new ideas. Our most valuable service innovations came not from my strategic planning but from frontline team members who felt empowered to suggest improvements.
- **Organizational resilience** strengthens under leadership that develops capabilities rather than dependencies. During market disruptions,

businesses with empowered teams adapt more quickly than those that wait for top-down direction.

The ultimate test of leadership comes when you are not present. A task manager's absence creates paralysis; a true leader's absence reveals an organization capable of not just maintaining but advancing toward the shared vision.

Empowering Your Team

Building Trust and Autonomy Within Your Team

The hardest leadership lesson I learned was that control and growth are mutually exclusive. My instinct to oversee every detail created a ceiling on our capacity and stifled the very talent I had hired. Building trust became not just a leadership virtue but a business necessity.

Trust begins with vulnerability, showing your team that you value their capabilities over your comfort. My breakthrough came when I allowed a team member to handle a major client presentation that I had always done myself. Despite my anxiety, she delivered better results than I typically did, connecting with the client in ways I hadn't.

Practical approaches for building trust include:

- **Delegating outcomes rather than just tasks.** Instead of prescribing exact methods, I define clear success parameters and give team members the authority to determine how to achieve them. This creates ownership while respecting their professional judgment.

- **Establishing appropriate safety nets.** Trust doesn't mean abandonment. I create review points for major projects and decision frameworks that provide guidance without micromanagement. This balance offers freedom within reasonable boundaries.
- **Consistently following through on commitments.** Trust flows both ways. When I promise resources, feedback, or support to my team, delivering reliably demonstrates that our relationship is built on mutual respect.
- **Addressing mistakes constructively.** How you respond when things go wrong determines whether trust grows or diminishes. I've learned to approach errors as learning opportunities rather than reasons to withdraw autonomy.

Encouraging Collaboration and Innovation

Individual empowerment creates capacity, but collaborative innovation multiplies it exponentially. The most valuable innovations in my business have emerged not from solitary brilliance but from the creative friction of diverse perspectives.

Foster a collaborative environment through intentional practices:

- **Create dedicated innovation spaces.** I schedule regular "possibility sessions" where the only agenda is to explore improvements and new approaches. These structured opportunities signal that innovation is expected, not just permitted.
- **Recognize collective achievements.** While individual recognition remains important, celebrating team accomplishments reinforces the idea that collaboration creates a greater impact than solo performance. I highlight innovations that emerged from cross-functional cooperation.
- **Implement cross-training and job shadowing.** Team members who understand each other's roles develop an appreciation for different perspectives and identify connection points for improvement. Some of our best process innovations have come from fresh eyes seeing familiar challenges.
- **Remove barriers to collaboration.** Physical separation, communication silos, and competitive incentives subtly discourage teamwork. I've redesigned both our office layout and compensation structure to reward collaborative outcomes over individual heroics.

The ultimate measure of empowerment isn't how the team performs when you're directing them; it's what they create when you're not even in the room. When I returned from a two-week absence to find that my team had developed and implemented a new client onboarding system that improved upon my original design, I knew our leadership evolution was working.

Creating a Positive Work Environment

Fostering Open Communication and Feedback

A positive work environment starts with communication that flows freely in all directions. Early in my leadership journey, I thought I had created an "open-door policy," but team members still hesitated to share their concerns or ideas. I eventually realized that psychological safety, not just physical accessibility, determines whether people feel safe to speak up.

Creating genuine open communication requires deliberate practices:

- **Model vulnerability first.** When I began openly sharing my own mistakes and uncertainties, team communication transformed. Acknowledging my missteps on a project set the tone that perfection wasn't expected and that honesty was valued over appearances.

- **Separate idea evaluation from idea generation.** I learned to respond to new suggestions with curiosity rather than immediate judgment. Simple phrases like "Tell me more about that" or "What excites you about this approach?" create space for ideas to develop before being evaluated.
- **Implement structured feedback mechanisms.** Beyond casual conversations, I established regular retrospectives where teams review what is working and what needs improvement. These formatted sessions normalize constructive feedback and ensure that quieter voices are heard.
- **Respond to feedback visibly.** Nothing kills communication faster than the sense that input disappears into a void. When team members raise concerns, I acknowledge them publicly and provide clear follow-up about the actions taken or decisions made.

Recognizing and Rewarding Contributions

Recognition isn't just a nice addition to leadership; it's essential fuel for sustained performance and engagement. I discovered this when team enthusiasm noticeably waned despite good business results. We were acknowledging outcomes but not the people creating them.

Effective recognition follows these principles:

- **Make it specific and timely.** Generic praise has limited impact. I focus on recognizing particular actions or qualities immediately rather than saving feedback for formal reviews. Specifically mentioning how someone's persistence solved a client problem carries more weight than general appreciation.
- **Align recognition with individual preferences.** Some team members thrive on public acknowledgment, while others prefer private appreciation. I maintain notes on each person's recognition preferences to ensure my approach resonates personally.
- **Celebrate the process, not just outcomes.** Recognizing effort, creativity, and collaboration-even when results fall short-reinforces the behaviors that drive long-term success. I make a point of highlighting exceptional work ethic or innovative thinking, regardless of immediate results.
- **Create peer recognition opportunities.** Some of the most meaningful appreciation comes from colleagues rather than leaders. Our "Spotlight" program enables team members to nominate peers for recognition, creating a culture where everyone participates in celebrating contributions.

The environment you create directly impacts what your team can achieve. Open communication ensures the best ideas surface, regardless of where they originate. Meaningful recognition ensures people bring their full energy and creativity to work. Together, they create a culture where people don't just perform; they thrive.

Leadership Traits for Sustainable Success

Developing Emotional Intelligence as a Leader

Technical expertise may have launched your business, but emotional intelligence determines how far your leadership can take it. I discovered this truth when facing a puzzling team dynamic: Despite clear direction and fair compensation, engagement was dropping. The missing element wasn't in our procedures but in my emotional awareness.

Emotional intelligence in leadership encompasses several critical capabilities:

- **Self-awareness** forms the foundation. I developed a practice of regularly checking in with my emotional state before key interactions. Recognizing when I was operating from frustration or anxiety allowed me to pause rather than let those emotions drive my decisions. This simple habit prevented countless counterproductive conversations.

- **Empathy** extends your perspective beyond your own experience. During a particularly challenging project, I noticed a normally enthusiastic team member becoming withdrawn. Rather than focusing solely on the deliverable, I made space to understand the personal challenges affecting her work. This conversation not only resolved the immediate situation but also deepened our working relationship.
- **Relationship management** transforms individual connections into team cohesion. I learned to recognize and navigate different communication styles, ensuring that introverts had space to contribute alongside more vocal team members. This attention to interpersonal dynamics unblocked creativity that had been stifled by dominant voices.
- **Emotional regulation** provides stability during turbulence. When our largest client unexpectedly departed, my initial reaction was panic. By recognizing and managing this response before communicating with the team, I was able to present the situation as an opportunity for realignment rather than as a disaster, setting a tone of determined optimism instead of fear.

The Importance of Adaptability and Resilience

The business landscape constantly shifts, making adaptability and resilience essential leadership traits. I learned this lesson during an economic downturn that threatened our core service model. The leaders who thrived weren't those with perfect forecasting but those who could adapt quickly to changing circumstances.

Cultivate these capabilities through intentional practices:

- **Develop scenario agility** by regularly considering multiple potential futures. I now guide my leadership team through quarterly scenario planning, where we identify emerging trends and develop response options. This mental rehearsal builds the flexibility to pivot when circumstances change.
- **Embrace productive discomfort** as a growth accelerator. Taking on challenging projects outside my expertise, such as implementing a new technology platform, strengthened my capacity to learn in uncertain situations. Each stretch experience built confidence that we could navigate unknown territory.
- **Maintain perspective during setbacks** by distinguishing between temporary challenges and existential threats. When we lost a major contract, I focused our team on the difference between a difficult quarter and a failed business. This perspective prevented panic reactions and allowed for thoughtful restructuring.

- **Build recovery rituals** that replenish your resilience. I discovered that my ability to lead through challenges directly correlated with my personal restoration practices. Regular physical activity, reflection time, and complete disconnection periods became non-negotiable elements of my schedule, particularly during difficult periods.

The most sustainable leaders aren't those who avoid difficulties but those who develop the emotional intelligence to navigate challenges while bringing others along with them. Your ability to understand yourself, connect with others, adapt to changing circumstances, and maintain resilience through adversity ultimately determines not just your business success but also your leadership legacy.

Inspiring Through Purpose

Vision without communication remains just a good idea trapped in your mind. I discovered this when my team was executing tasks efficiently but lacked the energy and initiative I hoped to see. The missing element wasn't competence or even motivation; it was purpose.

The Power of Clear Vision

Communicating vision isn't a one-time announcement but an ongoing practice of connecting everyday work to meaningful impact. Consider these approaches:

- **Use stories over statistics.** When launching a new service direction, I shared a client's transformation story rather than just the market opportunity. This narrative created an emotional connection to the purpose behind the initiative.
- **Simplify without diluting.** Our company vision initially spanned three paragraphs of carefully crafted language. Nobody remembered it. When we distilled it to a single compelling sentence, it began to appear naturally in team discussions. "We help business owners transform their relationship with their companies so they can transform their relationship with their lives."
- **Make vision visible.** Visual reminders throughout our workspace, client success photos, impact statements, and even relevant quotes, keep purpose present amid daily tasks.
- **Connect regularly to the bigger picture.** I start team meetings by sharing examples of how our work is fulfilling our purpose. These brief stories reconnect everyone to the meaning behind their efforts.

Creating Purpose Alignment

When team goals directly connect to the company's mission, motivation shifts from external pressure to internal drive. Here's how to build this alignment:

Include team members in the goal-setting process rather than simply assigning targets. When our client experience team participated in developing their service standards, their ownership and commitment dramatically increased.

Connect individual strengths to purpose fulfillment. During one-on-one meetings, I explore how each person's unique capabilities advance our mission. This personalized connection helps team members see themselves as essential to our purpose.

Celebrate purpose-aligned achievements specifically. When we celebrate successes, I stress not just what was accomplished but also how it advanced our goals.

This reinforcement helps to close the gap between daily employment and significant influence.

Revisit and refresh the connection regularly. Purpose can become background noise if not deliberately brought to the foreground. Quarterly purpose sessions, where we share client success stories and discuss how our work creates meaningful change, keep the mission alive.

Meaningful contributions to something greater than ourselves provide the most potent inspiration, not pressure or rewards. Team members who get not only what they are doing but also why it matters bring their whole creativity, enthusiasm, and dedication to their task.

As Antoine de Saint-Exupéry wisely noted, "If you want to build a ship, don't drum up people to collect wood and don't assign them tasks and work; rather, teach them to long for the endless immensity of the sea."

Steps to Evolve Your Leadership

Leadership evolution isn't accidental; it requires honest assessment and intentional development. My own path from a controlling manager to an empowering leader began with a simple question: "Is my leadership style helping or hindering our growth?"

Start With Honest Self-Assessment

Before you can evolve your leadership, you need to understand where you stand today:

- **Gather multidimensional feedback** from those who experience your leadership directly. I created a simple, anonymous survey asking team members about my strengths and areas for growth as a leader. Their insights revealed blind spots I couldn't see myself.
- **Identify your leadership triggers**, situations that prompt reactive rather than responsive leadership. I discovered that tight deadlines triggered my tendency to take over rather than coach, while

financial pressures activated my micromanagement instincts.

- **Examine the outcomes of your current approach.** Look beyond immediate results to the longer-term impacts on team development, innovation, and culture. I tracked how often team members brought forward new ideas, a direct reflection of whether my leadership was creating psychological safety.
- **Compare your espoused values with your actual behaviors.** I claimed to value autonomy while still requiring approval on decisions that team members were qualified to make. This gap between intention and action needed to be addressed.

Create Your Leadership Development Plan

With a clear understanding comes targeted growth:

- **Focus on high-leverage changes** that will create the greatest positive impact. Rather than trying to improve everything simultaneously, I prioritized developing my coaching skills, as this would most directly support team empowerment.
- **Seek development opportunities** suited to your learning style. While some leaders thrive in formal training, I found that working with a

leadership coach provided the personalized guidance and accountability I needed to evolve my approach.

- **Build new leadership habits** through consistent small practices. When team members brought problems to me, I developed the habit of asking, "What do you think we should do?" before offering solutions. This simple shift gradually transformed our interaction pattern.
- **Create accountability structures** to support your development. I shared my leadership goals with key team members, inviting them to call attention to moments when I reverted to old patterns. This transparency accelerated my growth while modeling continuous improvement.
- **Celebrate progress while acknowledging the journey.** Leadership evolution isn't a destination but an ongoing process. I recognize improvement without expecting perfection, using setbacks as opportunities to deepen my understanding rather than as reasons for discouragement.

The most powerful leadership transformation doesn't come from adopting external techniques but from internal shifts in how you see your role. As my perspective evolved from "I need to drive results through my team" to

"I need to develop a team capable of driving results," my leadership approach naturally followed.

Remember that your leadership directly shapes what is possible for your business. As you evolve from managing tasks to inspiring purpose and from controlling details to empowering initiative, you remove the ceiling on what your organization can achieve, and discover the leader you are truly capable of becoming.

CHAPTER 9

THE 90-DAY TRANSFORM

Knowledge without action creates little change. Throughout this book, we have explored powerful concepts for liberating your business and reclaiming your life; however, concepts alone will not transform your reality. What you need now is a structured path to implementation.

The 90-Day Transform provides exactly that, a practical framework for converting insights into tangible results. Rather than attempting to revolutionize everything at once, this approach focuses your energy on high-impact changes that are implemented systematically over three months.

In the pages that follow, I will guide you through the exact process I have used with hundreds of business owners to create meaningful, sustainable transformation, one deliberate step at a time.

The 90-Day Transform: Why 90 Days?

The Power of Short-Term, Focused Goals

Have you ever set ambitious annual goals in January only to find them forgotten by February? You're not alone. The traditional approach to business transformation, setting sweeping, year-long objectives, often fails because the timeframe is simply too long to maintain focus and momentum.

Ninety days strikes the perfect balance between immediate action and meaningful change. It's long enough to achieve substantial results yet short enough to create urgency and maintain engagement. When I work with business owners implementing the principles from this book, this timeframe consistently produces breakthroughs where longer horizons falter.

Short-term, focused goals create several distinct advantages:

- **Clarity and precision** become natural when working within a condensed timeframe. Rather than vague aspirations like "improve team communication," you are forced to define exactly what changes you will implement over the next 90 days. This specificity dramatically increases your likelihood of success.

- **Psychological momentum** builds as you experience early wins. Your brain rewards accomplishment with increased motivation, creating a positive cycle. Within just 2 to 3 weeks of focused effort, you will begin seeing tangible improvements that fuel your commitment to continue.
- **Resource allocation** becomes more effective with a concentrated focus. Instead of spreading your energy across numerous initiatives, the 90-day framework directs your attention to a few high-leverage changes, maximizing impact from limited time and resources.

How 90 Days Creates Momentum and Sustainable Change

The 90-day framework isn't just about short-term wins. It's designed to create lasting transformation through a carefully structured approach:

- **The first 30 days** focus on breaking patterns and establishing new foundations. This initial period often feels challenging as you disrupt comfortable habits and implement unfamiliar practices. By day 30, you'll have overcome the initial resistance and begun to establish new patterns.

- **The middle 30 days** build consistency and refinement. As new approaches become more familiar, your focus shifts from implementation to optimization. This middle period is when systems start functioning more smoothly, and team members adapt to changed expectations.
- **The final 30 days** solidify habits and prepare for expansion. By this point, your initial changes have taken root, allowing you to strengthen them while planning your next 90-day cycle. This continuous progression prevents the common pattern of regression after initial enthusiasm fades.

The power of this approach comes from its cyclical nature. Rather than being a one-time transformation attempt, the 90-Day Transform becomes a sustainable rhythm of constant evolution. Each cycle builds on the previous one, creating compound growth while maintaining manageable focus.

Instead of attempting a complete business reinvention, which almost inevitably fails due to overwhelming complexity, you'll implement focused changes that gradually transform your entire operation. Like compound interest, these seemingly modest 90-day improvements accumulate into remarkable transformations over time.

The 90-day timeframe also aligns perfectly with human psychology and business rhythms. It's long enough to push through the discomfort of change but short enough to maintain urgency and focus. It corresponds naturally with quarterly business planning while providing enough time to see meaningful results.

Step 1: Assess Your Starting Point

Identifying Current Challenges and Opportunities

Effective transformation begins with an honest assessment of your current reality. Without a clear understanding of your starting point, even well-intentioned changes may address the wrong problems or miss key opportunities.

Begin with a comprehensive business review focused on these key areas:

- **Time allocation** reveals where your energy actually goes versus where it should go. Track your activities for one week, categorizing each hour as strategic, operational, or reactive. Most business owners are shocked to discover that they spend less than 10% of their time on strategic activities that drive growth.
- **Systems assessment** identifies which business processes are working smoothly and which create friction. Evaluate your client acquisition, service delivery, team management, and financial processes. Look specifically for bottlenecks that consistently require your personal attention.

- **Team dynamics** determine how effectively your business can function without you. Assess your team's current autonomy, decision-making confidence, and problem-solving capabilities. Note areas where team members consistently seek your input rather than take ownership.
- **Personal alignment** measures how well your business currently supports your life priorities. Consider your stress levels, work hours, ability to disconnect, and overall satisfaction. Be brutally honest about whether your business is enhancing or diminishing your quality of life.

The goal isn't just to identify problems but also to recognize hidden opportunities. Often, the most significant transformation comes not from fixing what's broken but from leveraging what's already working well.

Setting a Baseline for Progress

Transformation becomes meaningful only when measured against a clear starting point. Establish specific baselines in both quantitative and qualitative dimensions

Quantitative measures provide objective data points for comparison:

- Hours worked per week
- Number of decisions requiring your input
- Response time to client requests
- Revenue per employee
- Personal time off taken

Qualitative indicators capture the subjective elements of your business reality:

- Stress levels and overall well-being
- Team satisfaction and engagement
- Quality of client relationships
- Your personal fulfillment and energy

Document these baseline measurements thoroughly, as they will serve as your reference point throughout the transformation process. I recommend creating a simple dashboard with your key metrics, making it easy to track progress over the coming weeks.

Remember that assessment isn't just a preliminary step; it's an ongoing practice. Schedule brief weekly reviews throughout your 90-day journey to track progress and identify emerging challenges or opportunities.

This consistent monitoring allows you to adjust your approach rather than discovering on day 90 that you've been moving in the wrong direction.

Step 2: Define Your Priorities

Aligning Goals With Your Vision and Values

With a clear understanding of your starting point, the next critical step is to ensure that your 90-day goals connect directly to your larger vision and core values. Without this alignment, you risk achieving objectives that ultimately do not create meaningful change in your business and life.

Begin by revisiting your fundamental purpose:

- Why did you originally start this business?
- What impact do you want to create for your clients, team members, and yourself?
- What kind of life do you want your business to support?

This reconnection with your deeper purpose provides the compass for your 90-day journey. When I neglected this step during an early transformation attempt, I successfully implemented new systems that increased efficiency but discovered that they were taking the business in a direction that did not actually align with my values or vision.

Now, test potential goals against your vision and values by asking:

- Will this change move me toward my vision, or will it just solve a temporary problem?
- Does this priority honor my core values, or does it compromise them?
- Am I choosing this goal because it matters deeply or because it seems urgent?

True transformation comes from addressing root causes, not just symptoms. For instance, if you are working excessive hours, the symptom is time scarcity, but the root cause might be inadequate systems, poor boundaries, or even a business model that fundamentally requires your constant involvement.

Choosing Key Focus Areas for the Next 90 Days

The most common mistake in transformation efforts is trying to change too much at once. Effective change requires focused energy. For your 90-Day Transform, select a maximum of three priorities that will create the greatest positive impact.

Use these criteria to identify your highest-leverage opportunities:

- Which changes would create a ripple effect, positively impacting multiple areas?
- What improvements would remove the most significant barriers to your vision?
- Which priorities would address root causes rather than symptoms?
- What changes are you genuinely committed to implementing, rather than just being interested in?

Based on my experience guiding hundreds of business transformations, these focus areas consistently deliver the highest return on effort:

- **Systemizing your most time-consuming operational processes** frees up capacity for strategic work while reducing your business's dependency on your personal involvement.
- **Developing decisive leadership within your team** multiplies your impact by creating the capability to handle decisions and challenges without your constant input.
- **Implementing clear boundaries between work and personal life** enhances both business

performance and quality of life through improved focus and renewal.

- **Creating a streamlined client experience** often simultaneously improves client results, team efficiency, and profitability-a rare triple win.

Once you've selected your priorities, define specific, measurable outcomes for each. Rather than stating "improve team communication," target "implement a structured weekly meeting rhythm that reduces reactive communications by 50%."

Step 3: Create an Action Plan

Breaking Down Big Goals Into Manageable Steps

Even the most inspiring goals remain dreams without a concrete plan for implementation. The key to turning your priorities into reality lies in breaking them down into clear, actionable steps.

Start by identifying the major milestones for each of your priorities. For example, if your goal is to implement a new client management system, your milestones might include:

- Researching and selecting appropriate software.
- Configuring system settings and workflows.
- Migrating existing client data.

- Training the team on new processes.
- Fully transitioning client management to the new system.

For each milestone, define what "done" looks like. Specific completion criteria eliminate ambiguity and allow you to track genuine progress. Rather than using vague targets like "improve team training," define exactly what successful completion entails: "Create and deliver structured training sessions covering all system functions, with team members demonstrating independent use of key features."

Next, sequence these milestones in logical order, noting dependencies where one step must be completed before another can begin. This creates your critical path, the sequence of actions necessary to achieve your goal within the 90-day timeframe.

Finally, assign realistic timeframes to each milestone, working backward from your 90-day endpoint. Building in buffer time for unexpected challenges prevents the common pattern of timeline slippage that undermines transformation efforts.

Setting Weekly and Daily Tasks for Progress

The bridge between 90-day goals and daily action is weekly planning. At the beginning of each week, review your milestone map and identify the specific tasks needed to make progress toward your next milestone.

Create a weekly action plan that specifies:

- Which tasks will be completed this week
- Who is responsible for each task
- What resources are needed
- How completion will be verified

Then, translate these weekly priorities into daily action items. Each day, identify the 2-3 most important tasks that will move your transformation forward. Complete these priority tasks before addressing routine operational matters. This discipline ensures that important but non-urgent transformation work does not get displaced by the constant stream of daily urgencies.

Protect designated implementation time in your calendar-block 60–90 minutes daily specifically for your transformation priorities. Without this scheduled commitment, urgent matters will consistently displace important transformation work.

The most effective implementation combines disciplined action with regular reflection. At the end of each week, review your progress against planned milestones. This weekly checkpoint allows you to:

- Celebrate completed actions.
- Identify and address obstacles.
- Adjust upcoming plans based on lessons learned.
- Maintain momentum through visible progress.

Step 4: Build Accountability

Establishing Accountability Systems for Yourself and Your Team

Even the most carefully crafted plans falter without proper accountability. Willpower alone rarely sustains transformation; you need structured systems that keep you and your team focused on your priorities when the initial enthusiasm inevitably wanes.

Start by creating different layers of accountability:

- **Personal accountability** begins with clear commitments to yourself. I maintain a daily "transformation scorecard" where I track whether I have completed my priority actions each day. This simple practice creates internal accountability through consistent self-monitoring.
- **Partner accountability** adds external perspective and support. Identify someone who will hold you to your commitments, whether a business coach, trusted colleague, or accountability partner. Schedule regular check-ins to review progress, discuss challenges, and recommit to your priorities.
- **Team accountability** extends responsibility beyond yourself. Share relevant aspects of your 90-day plan with your team, clearly communicating how their actions contribute to the larger

transformation. Regular team huddles focused specifically on transformation priorities prevent these initiatives from being displaced by daily operations.

- **Structural accountability** embeds your commitments into your environment and routines. Block implementation time in your calendar, create visible progress trackers in your workspace, and establish regular review points in your weekly schedule.

The most effective accountability combines supportive encouragement with direct challenges. When I work with transformation clients, I balance celebrating their progress with asking uncomfortable questions about missed commitments or avoided challenges.

Tracking Progress and Adjusting as Needed

Effective transformation requires not just initial planning but also continuous monitoring and adjustment. Establish a rhythm of regular reviews at different intervals:

- **Daily check-ins** (5–10 minutes) to review priority tasks and identify immediate obstacles. I use a simple end-of-day practice, asking, "Did I complete my priority actions today? If not, what prevented it, and how will I adjust tomorrow?"
- **Weekly reviews** (30–60 minutes) to assess milestone progress and plan for the coming week. Each

Friday, I evaluate what worked, what didn't, and what adjustments are needed to maintain momentum.

- **Monthly deep dives** (2–3 hours) to evaluate over-all transformation progress. These more extensive reviews include comparing current metrics to the baseline, identifying emerging patterns, and making larger adjustments to the approach if needed.

Use these review points to practice "flexible persistence," maintaining commitment to your priorities while adapting your methods based on what is working and what isn't. The goal isn't to perfectly execute your original plan but to achieve the transformation it was designed to create. Create simple tracking tools that provide clear visibility into your progress. Visual indicators like milestone charts, progress thermometers, or simple red/yellow/green status indicators make it easy to see at a glance where you stand. These visible reminders help maintain focus and create natural accountability.

Step 5: Measure Success Beyond Numbers

Identifying Metrics That Reflect Real Progress

Traditional business metrics, revenue, profit, and growth rates, tell only part of the transformation story. True success extends far beyond financial indicators to encompass the quality of your business and life.

Create a holistic measurement framework that captures success across multiple dimensions:

- **Freedom metrics** track your personal liberation from operational demands. Measure hours worked, vacation days taken without interruption, and time spent on strategic versus tactical activities. One client discovered that while her revenue had increased only modestly during her 90-day transformation, her personal workload had decreased by 15 hours weekly, a success that is invisible in traditional financial reports.
- **Capacity indicators** measure your business's ability to function without your constant involvement. Track the percentage of decisions made without your input, client matters handled independently by your team, and operational processes that run smoothly without your oversight.
- **Well-being measures** assess the human impact of your transformation. Monitor your stress levels, sleep quality, and energy. One simple approach is to rate your satisfaction across key life areas on a 1–10 scale weekly, tracking improvements over time.
- **Relationship quality** often reveals deeper transformation progress. Has your presence and engagement with family improved? Are your client and team relationships more fulfilling? These

qualitative shifts may not appear in financial statements but fundamentally define successful transformation.

The most revealing metrics often emerge from your specific priorities. If your goal was to implement team decision frameworks, measure not just whether the framework exists but also how often it is successfully used. If you aimed to create client onboarding systems, track both the completion of implementation and the resulting impact on client satisfaction and team efficiency.

Celebrating Milestones and Recognizing Achievements

Transformation is challenging work. Without deliberate celebration, the focus remains on what is still unfinished rather than on what has been accomplished. Create intentional recognition practices to maintain motivation and momentum:

- **Scheduled celebrations** mark significant milestones. When we completed our client management system implementation, we held a team lunch specifically to recognize this achievement before immediately moving on to the next priority.
- **Visual progress indicators** provide a constant reminder of how far you have come. Simple tools

like milestone charts with completed items crossed off or before-and-after metrics create visible evidence of progress.

- **Team recognition** acknowledges everyone's contributions to the transformation. Specific praise for individual efforts builds collective ownership of the journey and reinforces the behaviors that drive positive change.
- **Personal rewards** create meaningful incentives aligned with your values. After completing a particularly challenging phase of my own business transformation, I took my first completely unplugged three-day weekend in years, a reward that reinforced the very freedom I was working to create.

Remember that transformation is never "finished." It is an ongoing journey of evolution. The completion of your 90-day plan is not an endpoint but a platform from which to launch your next phase of growth. Celebrate your progress while maintaining the habits and systems that created it.

Maintaining Momentum After 90 Days

Reflecting on Lessons Learned During the Process

The completion of your 90-Day Transform isn't just an endpoint; it's a powerful learning opportunity that shapes your future growth. Take time for structured reflection that captures insights while they are fresh.

Begin by reviewing your journey objectively. What worked? What didn't? Where did you encounter unexpected obstacles or discover surprising strengths? I maintain a "lessons learned" journal throughout transformation periods, noting specific insights as they emerge. This practice creates a valuable resource for future planning.

Look for patterns in your implementation experience:

- Which types of changes were implemented most successfully?
- Where did you consistently encounter resistance?
- What support mechanisms proved most valuable?
- Which priorities maintained momentum, and which lost steam?

These patterns reveal important insights about your personal working style, team dynamics, and organizational culture. One client discovered that initiatives involving direct client experience consistently gained traction, while internal operational changes frequently stalled. This pattern helped her design more effective implementation strategies for future transformations.

Document both your successes and challenges honestly. Transformation isn't about perfect execution but about meaningful progress and learning. The obstacles you encountered provide valuable data for designing your next 90-day cycle.

Setting the Stage for Continued Growth and Success

The greatest risk after completing your 90-Day Transform is reverting to old patterns. Protect your progress by creating structures that maintain momentum:

- **Establish your next 90-day horizon** immediately. Don't wait until the current cycle ends to begin planning the next. I typically start designing my next transformation focus when I am approximately 75 days into the current cycle, ensuring continuity of progress.
- **Build maintenance systems** for your newly established practices. What monitoring, reinforcement, or regular attention is needed to preserve the changes you have implemented? New habits and systems often deteriorate without deliberate maintenance, especially in the first few months after implementation.
- **Deepen successful changes** rather than constantly pursuing new initiatives. Often, the most valuable next step is not implementing additional changes but strengthening and expanding your most successful transformations. My most effective

client transformed her client onboarding process in her first 90 days, then focused her second cycle on refining and enhancing this system rather than tackling an entirely new area.

- **Create a continuous transformation rhythm** that becomes part of your business culture. Establish regular quarterly planning sessions that identify opportunities for focused improvement. This ongoing cycle prevents the common pattern of sporadic, reactive change followed by long periods of stagnation.

The ultimate measure of transformation success is simple: Is your business increasingly becoming a vehicle for the life you want rather than an obstacle to it? With each thoughtfully designed and implemented 90-day cycle, you move closer to the freedom and impact that inspired your entrepreneurial journey in the first place.

CHAPTER 10

THE FUTURE OF YOUR FREEDOM

We've covered a lot of ground throughout this book, from breaking free of the ownership trap to implementing transformative systems and evolving your leadership. However, this journey isn't just about where you've been; it's about where you're going.

In this final chapter, we'll look beyond immediate challenges to the lasting impact you can create. Your business isn't just a vehicle for generating income; it's an opportunity to build something meaningful that reflects your deepest values and serves your highest aspirations.

Let's explore how to shape a future where your business becomes not just successful but also significant, creating a legacy worthy of your life's work.

The Future of Your Freedom

Reflecting on Your Journey and Growth

Take a moment to acknowledge how far you've come. Whether you've implemented every strategy in this book or have just begun making small changes, you have started the journey from business owner to business leader. That shift, from being owned by your business to truly owning it, represents profound growth.

I remember the moment I realized my own transformation had taken root. I was on vacation, and for the first time in years, I hadn't checked my email once in three days. Even more telling was that I wasn't anxious about what might be happening in my absence. The systems we had built were working. The team was handling challenges. The business was serving clients effectively without my constant oversight.

This freedom didn't happen overnight. It came through the accumulated impact of many deliberate choices, saying no to certain opportunities, investing time in system development rather than just task completion, and empowering team members even when it felt risky.

Your journey may look different, but the growth you experience will be equally meaningful. Take time to recognize the shifts in how you think, work, and lead. These changes aren't just professional developments; they are personal transformations that impact every aspect of your life.

The Importance of Vision in Long-Term Success

Freedom without direction quickly becomes aimless wandering. As you create space in your business and life, the question becomes: What will you do with that freedom? This is where vision becomes essential.

Your vision serves as the North Star, guiding all your business decisions, from daily priorities to long-term strategy. It answers fundamental questions: Why does this business exist beyond making money? What impact do we seek to create? How will the world be different because of our work?

A compelling vision has the following characteristics:

- It inspires action rather than merely describing outcomes.
- It connects to genuine values rather than simply sounding impressive.
- It provides clear direction while allowing for flexible implementation.
- It serves as a filter for opportunities and decisions.

Most importantly, an effective vision extends beyond business metrics to encompass the life you want to create. My own vision includes not only building a successful company but also using that company as a vehicle to demonstrate that business success and personal fulfillment can reinforce, rather than compete with, each other.

Your vision will evolve as you grow. What matters is that it authentically reflects what truly matters to you, not what you think should matter based on others' expectations. This real vision becomes the basis for building not only a profitable company but also a legacy.

Defining Your Legacy

What Do You Want to Be Remembered For?

Legacy thinking shifts your perspective from quarterly results to generational impact. It poses a profound question: when your business journey is complete, what will remain?

I confronted this question after a health scare forced me to consider what I would leave behind if my time were suddenly cut short. The initial answer was uncomfortable: a successful business that would likely dissolve without me, as it revolved around my personal expertise and relationships. That realization sparked a fundamental shift in how I approached my work.

Legacy isn't just about what happens after you're gone; it shapes how you operate today.

Ask yourself:

- Who are the people whose lives you want to impact?
- What problems or needs do you feel called to address?
- What principles do you want your business to embody?
- What knowledge or wisdom do you want to pass on?

Your responses expose not only what you wish to leave behind but also what should direct your present decisions. A clear legacy vision helps you distinguish between what is merely profitable and what is truly meaningful.

Aligning Your Business With Your Personal Values

A business that contradicts your personal values creates internal conflict that eventually undermines both performance and fulfillment. Authentic alignment between who you are and how your business operates fosters both sustainable success and personal satisfaction.

Start by identifying your core values, not generic business virtues, but the genuine principles that guide your life decisions. For me, these include authenticity, growth, service, and balance. Then, honestly assess how well your current business practices reflect these values.

Where misalignments exist, make deliberate choices to bring your business into harmony with your values:

- Reshape your client experience to reflect how you genuinely want to serve others.
- Modify your team culture to embody how you believe people should be treated.
- Adjust your growth strategy to align with your authentic priorities.
- Revise your definition of success to include what truly matters to you.

This alignment isn't just personally satisfying; it's strategically powerful. When your business authentically reflects your values, decision-making becomes clearer, team culture grows stronger, and client relationships deepen. Your unique values become a genuine competitive advantage that cannot be easily replicated.

The most meaningful legacy emerges not from following conventional business wisdom but from building an enterprise that authentically embodies who you are and what you believe.

Planning for Sustainability

Creating Systems That Support Long-Term Growth

Sustainable growth requires systems that can expand without breaking. Too often, businesses build processes that work for their current size but collapse under the pressure of growth, creating cycles of progress and regression that drain resources and enthusiasm.

Future-focused systems share key characteristics:

- **Scalability** means your processes can handle increasing volume without proportional increases in complexity or resources. Design systems with growth parameters in mind from the beginning. I learned this lesson when our client onboarding process, which worked beautifully for 20 clients, became a bottleneck at 50 clients, requiring a complete redesign during our busiest period.
- **Adaptability** allows your systems to evolve as your business changes. Create modular processes where components can be modified without disrupting the entire framework. Enable deliberate evolution rather than accidental breakage by documenting not only the functionality of systems but also the rationale behind their design.
- **Simplicity** ensures that systems remain manageable as you grow. Complexity may seem sophisticated, but it creates fragility. I've found that simple, well-executed processes consistently outperform complicated ones, especially during growth phases when resources are stretched.

- **Documentation** transforms systems from person-dependent to process-dependent. Thoroughly document your core processes so they can be maintained and expanded by anyone with appropriate training, not just by their original creator.

Building a Business That Thrives Without You

The ultimate test of business sustainability is simple: Would it continue to thrive if you stepped away? Creating this level of independence requires deliberate design.

Start by building distributed leadership, developing multiple team members capable of making decisions aligned with your vision and values. This depth of leadership provides resilience against the departure of any individual, including yourself.

Create knowledge redundancy so that critical information does not reside with a single individual. Cross-training, documentation, and transparent information sharing ensure that the business does not depend on any one person's knowledge.

Implement governance structures that provide guidance without requiring your constant presence. Clear decision frameworks, well-defined values, and established operating principles allow the organization to maintain direction even when you are not there to provide it.

Focus on building an owner-independent value proposition. If client relationships depend primarily on you, the business remains fundamentally vulnerable. Develop service delivery models and team capabilities that create value clients appreciate, regardless of your personal involvement.

Leaving an Impact

How to Empower Your Team to Continue the Vision

Your vision's longevity depends on how deeply it resides within your team. A vision that remains primarily in your head and heart will fade when you step back, while one embedded in your team's thinking and actions will flourish regardless of your presence.

Effective vision transfer requires more than occasional inspirational talks or printed mission statements; it occurs through consistent practices:

- **Share the why behind decisions**, not just the what. When team members understand the reasoning behind choices, they develop the ability to make similar decisions independently. I make a point of explaining not just what we're doing but why it aligns with our vision, creating a decision-making framework that others can apply.

- **Involve team members in vision refinement** so they become co-creators rather than just followers. Our annual vision sessions include representatives from all levels of the organization, ensuring that diverse perspectives shape our direction while building collective ownership.
- **Connect daily work to a larger purpose** by regularly highlighting how specific tasks and projects advance the vision. These relationships allow team members to consider their roles as contributions to something larger than themselves.
- **Celebrate vision-aligned behaviors** to reinforce the culture you're building. Recognition is a powerful teacher, what you acknowledge and appreciate becomes what your team values and repeats.

Fostering a Culture of Innovation and Collaboration

A sustainable legacy requires a culture that can adapt and evolve after you are gone. Static organizations preserve the letter of their founders' vision while losing its spirit. Dynamic cultures maintain core principles while continuously finding new expressions.

Build innovation into your organizational DNA by creating the following conditions:

- **Psychological safety** ensures that people can suggest new ideas without fear of criticism or punishment. When a team member proposed a radical change to our client service model, we explored it thoroughly rather than dismissing it, even though it challenged our established approach.

- **Structured creativity** provides frameworks for innovation rather than leaving it to chance. Regular innovation sessions, cross-functional problem-solving teams, and formal channels for improvement suggestions systematize your approach to evolution.
- **Collaborative problem-solving** leverages diverse perspectives to create better solutions than any individual could develop alone. Create decision-making processes that intentionally incorporate multiple viewpoints and areas of expertise.
- **Learning orientation** treats mistakes as valuable data rather than failures to be punished. This approach encourages reasonable risk-taking and experimentation, which are essential elements of adaptive organizations.

An organization that knows how to innovate and collaborate will continue evolving long after your direct involvement ends, perhaps the most powerful legacy you can leave.

Balancing Ambition With Fulfillment

Setting Future Goals That Reflect Personal and Professional Harmony

Ambitious goals drive growth, but not all growth enhances the quality of life. The entrepreneurial world often celebrates expansion metrics, revenue increases, market share gains, and team size growth, without questioning whether these advances actually create the life you want.

True success integrates professional achievement with personal fulfillment rather than sacrificing one for the other. Set future goals that honor both dimensions:

- **Define success holistically** by identifying what "enough" looks like across multiple areas. I maintain a personal dashboard with targets for business performance, personal time, health metrics, and relationship quality. This comprehensive view prevents business ambitions from overshadowing other priorities.
- **Create integrated goals** that advance both business and personal aspirations simultaneously. For example, developing stronger team leadership doesn't just build business capacity; it creates the personal freedom for family time and renewal.
- **Apply the "10-year test"** to major decisions. When considering significant business moves, ask

yourself, "How will I feel about this choice a decade from now?" This perspective often reveals the difference between opportunities that support your broader life vision and those that merely advance business metrics.

Avoiding the Trap of Constant Growth at the Expense of Well-Being

The entrepreneurial narrative often portrays perpetual expansion as the only acceptable path. This unexamined growth imperative drives many business owners to sacrifice health, relationships, and fulfillment on the altar of constant advancement.

Sustainable success requires a more nuanced approach:

- **Distinguish between growth and scale.** Growth often means doing more of the same, which requires proportional increases in resources and effort. Scaling means creating more impact without corresponding increases in personal bandwidth. I have intentionally focused on scaling our impact rather than merely growing our size.
- **Recognize business seasons.** Not every period demands expansion. Sometimes, consolidation, refinement, or even strategic contraction better serves both business health and personal well-being.

Building this cyclical understanding into your planning prevents the exhaustion that comes from constant pushing.

- **Practice sufficiency alongside ambition.** Regularly ask, "What's enough?" Defining parameters for sufficient income, market presence, and business complexity creates the freedom to optimize for quality of life alongside business metrics.
- **Build renewal into your ambition.** The most sustainable high achievers integrate periods of intense focus with genuine recovery. I schedule quarterly renewal retreats during which I completely disconnect from operations to restore perspective and energy.

Continuing the Journey

Embracing Growth as a Lifelong Process

The journey toward business freedom and personal fulfillment isn't a destination you reach only once; rather, it is a path you travel continuously. The most successful business owners understand that growth, both personal and professional, never truly ends.

This mindset shift from "arriving" to "evolving" brings profound benefits. When I stopped seeing freedom as a fixed endpoint and started viewing it as an ongoing practice, my experience of business ownership transformed. Each challenge became not an obstacle to freedom but an opportunity to develop greater capacity.

Treat your development as a lifelong commitment by:

- **Seeking continuous learning** through diverse sources. I maintain a regular reading practice across business, psychology, leadership, and completely unrelated fields that spark fresh thinking. This cross-disciplinary approach generates insights that no single domain could provide.
- **Finding developmental peers** who challenge your thinking and support your growth. My monthly mastermind group provides perspective, accountability, and encouragement far beyond what I could create alone.
- **Establishing regular reflection practices** that help you integrate experiences into wisdom. Without deliberate reflection, experience alone doesn't guarantee growth. Monthly reviews of what I'm learning, where I'm struggling, and how I'm evolving turn challenges into development.

Staying Open to Change and New Opportunities

The business landscape continuously evolves, rendering yesterday's formulas increasingly less effective. To be successful in the long term, you need to do more than just apply what you've learned. You also need to be open to new opportunities.

Cultivate openness through these practices:

- **Maintain a beginner's mind** even as you develop expertise. The most innovative leaders combine deep knowledge with genuine curiosity. Regularly ask questions that challenge your assumptions: "What if the opposite were true?" "What would someone from a completely different industry do here?"
- **Create space for emergence** rather than filling every moment with activity. Some of my most valuable business insights emerged during periods of genuine white space, time without a specific agenda or outcome. Build margin into your schedule for the unexpected connections and ideas that arise only in stillness.
- **View endings as beginnings.** Business cycles naturally include completion phases. Services become obsolete, markets shift, and seasons change. Rather than clinging to what's familiar, approach these transitions with curiosity about what might emerge next.

The true entrepreneur's journey isn't just about building a successful business. It's about becoming the person capable of creating success aligned with your deepest values. Accepting that progress is a permanent process and staying open to it, you change not only your business but also yourself.

This book isn't an endpoint but a beginning. The principles, practices, and possibilities we've explored together are simply tools for your ongoing journey toward greater freedom, impact, and fulfillment. The path continues, and the best is yet to come.

YOUR NEXT STEP

Picture this: You're sitting at your desk, not burning the midnight oil, but wrapping up at a reasonable hour. Your phone isn't blowing up with client emergencies. Your team has handled today's challenges beautifully without you. And tomorrow? You're taking the day off without a hint of anxiety.

This isn't fantasy; it's what freedom looks like. If I could journey from bankruptcy and burnout to building a business that truly works, I promise you can too.

Throughout this book, we've tackled the real struggles that entrepreneurship brings: the ownership trap that keeps you working IN your business instead of ON it, the systems that free you from daily operations, the leadership evolution that transforms both your team and yourself, and the boundaries that protect what matters most.

But knowledge without action is just entertainment. The difference between entrepreneurs who transform their relationship with their business and those who remain trapped isn't what they know; it's what they implement.

So, what's your next step?

Maybe it's documenting that process that's currently stuck in your head. Perhaps it's having that difficult conversation with a client about boundaries. Or it could be identifying your first delegation opportunity. Whatever you choose, start now. Not when things "slow down" (spoiler alert: they won't). Not when you feel completely ready (you never will). Begin today with one small but significant step toward the business and life you deserve.

Will it be perfect? Absolutely not. My own journey had plenty of detours, setbacks, and moments when I wondered if it was all worth it. But each step forward, however imperfect, brought me closer to freedom.

Remember the Uber Eats receipts I mentioned at the beginning of this book? Those $1,100 in takeout orders weren't just about food; they reflected a life that had spun out of control. Today, my spending (and my life) looks dramatically different. Not because I became perfect, but because I built systems and boundaries that support making better choices.

Your journey to business freedom isn't about achieving perfection. It's about progress, about creating a business that serves your life instead of consuming it, about building something that reflects your values and supports your vision.

You already have everything you need to begin. The fact that you've read this far proves you have the determination. The strategies in these pages provide the roadmap. And I believe with absolute certainty that you have what it takes to create a business that works for your life, not against it.

Your freedom journey starts now, and I can't wait to see where it takes you.

GLOSSARY

Burnout Cycle: The repeating pattern of overwork, exhaustion, and recovery that traps many entrepreneurs in a state of perpetual stress.

Decision Matrix: A framework that defines which decisions team members can make independently versus those that require consultation or approval.

Delegation Framework: A systematic approach to transferring responsibilities and authority to team members effectively.

Freedom Framework: A comprehensive system for building a business that operates without the owner's constant involvement.

Growth vs. Scale: Growth increases revenue by adding proportional resources, while scaling increases revenue without proportional resource increases.

Leadership Evolution: The progression from a hands-on operator to a strategic leader who inspires and empowers others.

Ownership Trap: The condition in which a business owner becomes essential to daily operations, leading to burnout and limited growth.

Process Playbook: Documented workflows and procedures that enable team members to execute tasks consistently.

Psychological Safety: A team environment in which members feel safe to take risks, speak up, and make mistakes without fear of punishment.

Systems-Dependent: A business that operates based on documented processes rather than relying on specific individuals.

90-Day Transform: A focused implementation approach that uses 90-day cycles to create sustainable business change.

Work-Life Harmony: The integration of professional and personal priorities in a way that supports both simultaneously, rather than treating them as competing interests.

ACKNOWLEDGEMENTS

To my sons, Prince and Dylan this journey has always belonged to the three of us. Thank you for your patience with the late nights, your grace in the growing pains, and your steady love through every season. You've been my why, my grounding, and the quiet strength behind everything I've built.

Prince, thank you for being my first experience of motherhood and my daily reminder to lead with courage. Your heart, your protectiveness, and the way you rise to responsibility inspire me more than you know.

Dylan, thank you for your light, your laughter, and the joy you bring into our home. You remind me to stay present, to keep it playful, and to believe in what's possible even when things feel heavy.

To my clients and colleagues: thank you for trusting me, referring me, and opening doors when I couldn't get them elsewhere. Your belief created opportunities that changed my life and I will always honor that trust by doing the work with excellence.

ABOUT THE AUTHOR

Kelli Lewis is an accountant, business strategist, and founder of KelliWorks®, where she helps entrepreneurs create clarity, structure, and sustainable success without burning out. With two decades of experience in accounting and operations, she blends deep financial expertise with a grounded, human-centered approach to leadership and business growth.

After building a thriving firm from the ground up while raising two sons as a single mother, Kelli knows firsthand what it means to push past exhaustion and lose yourself in the process. Her own journey through overwork and self-realignment fuels her mission to help business owners build companies that support their lives instead of consuming them.

Widely recognized for her practical, compassionate guidance, Kelli empowers founders to create systems that bring freedom, focus, and peace of mind. When she isn't helping entrepreneurs transform the way they work, she's spending time with her sons or connecting with the growing community inside Entrepreneurs Anonymous.

Let's Stay Connected

If this book hit home, your next step is community.
Join Entrepreneurs Anonymous (EA) to stay supported with biweekly calls, structure, and accountability, so you don't slide back into isolation and overwhelm.

Join now:
Entrepreneuranonymous.net
Or
Kelliworks.com

REFERENCES

Analysing the current business situation. (2023). Goal-Envision. https://goalenvision.com/knowledge-bank/ analysing-the-current-business-situation

Automation or Delegation? A Framework for How to Figure Out What Processes In Your Agency Should Be Delegated vs. Automated. (2023, December 13). *HighLevel.* https://blog.gohighlevel.com/automation-or-delegation-a-framework-for-how-to-figure-out-what-processes-in-your-agency-should-be-delegated-vs-automated/

Avolio, H. (2024, November 15). *From Frenzy to Focus: How We Can Cancel Hustle Culture And Create A New Sustainable Work Paradigm.* Her Nation Magazine. https://www.hernationmagazine.com/post/from-frenzy-to-focus-how-we-can-cancel-hustle-culture-and-create-a-new-sustainable-work-paradigm

Bartes, B. (2024, August 12). Are *You Working On Your Business Or In Your Business?* Forbes. https://www.forbes.com/councils/forbescoachescouncil/2024/08/12/are-you-working-on-your-business-or-in-your-business/

Bosworth, P. (2023, August 30). *The Future of Leadership is Collaborative Leadership Choice*. Leadership Choice. https://www.leadershipchoice.com/future-of-leadership-is-collaborative/

Brooks, E. (2024). *Overcoming the Fear of Delegation*. Virtuallybrooks.com. https://doi.org/10/2024/08/The-Role-of-Virtual-Assistants-in-Managing-Your-Online-Presence-2-1024x576

Chandra, D. (2024, December 3). How To Create Systems In Your Business: The Process Hacker Way. *The Process Hacker*. https://theprocesshacker.com/blog/how-to-create-systems/

Chevannes, S.(2023, September 01). *Mastering Self-Care: A Guide For Entrepreneurs*. Forbes. https://www.forbes.com/councils/forbesbusinesscouncil/2023/09/01/mastering-self-care-a-guide-for-entrepreneurs/

Dekel, R. (2024, December 24). *The 5 Fears Every Entrepreneur Must Face - and Overcome*. Entrepreneur. https://www.entrepreneur.com/starting-a-business/the-5-fears-every-entrepreneur-must-face-and-overcome/482028

Deveaux, M. (2022, September 16). *90-Day Plan: Benefits, Planning, and Potential Pitfalls*. Marie Deveaux. https://mariedeveaux.com/2022/09/16/90-day-plan-benefits-planning-and-potential-pitfalls/

Fink, H. (2025). *28 Best Process Automation Software Reviewed in 2025*. The Digital Project Manager. https://doi.org/1090842/fonts-486d8047c7ba9f1d1a9708e36f985493

Fletcher, D. P. (2020, November 13). *Work-Life Balance Is Over: Let's Talk About Work-Life Harmony*. Forbes. https://www.forbes.com/councils/forbeshumanresourcescouncil/2020/11/13/work-life-balance-is-over-lets-talk-about-work-life-harmony/

Forbes Coaches Council (2021, March 19). *Torn Between Working On Or In The Business? 11 Ways To Strike A Balance*. Forbes. https://www.forbes.com/councils/forbescoachescouncil/2021/03/19/torn-between-working-on-or-in-the-business-11-ways-to-strike-a-balance/

Gannon, B. (2021, August 23). *Why Boundaries Are So Important For Entrepreneurs (And How To Have More Of Them)*. Forbes. https://www.forbes.com/

councils/forbesbusinesscouncil/2021/08/23/why-boundaries-are-so-important-for-entrepreneurs-and-how-to-have-more-of-them/

Greves, D. (2023, November 21). *The Power of Scaling: Implementing Business Operating Systems for Sustainable Growth*. KB Growth Advisory. https://kbgrowthadvisory.com/the-power-of-scaling-implementing-business-operating-systems-for-sustainable-growth/

Hall, J. (2024, October 18). Time is Money: A Guide to Effective Time Management for Entrepreneurs. *Calendar*. https://www.calendar.com/blog/time-is-money-a-guide-to-effective-time-management-for-entrepreneurs/

Henderson, J. (2024, November 14). *Is Your Team Thriving or Just Surviving? 5 Long-Term Strategies to Build and Sustain High-Performing Teams*. Entrepreneur. https://www.entrepreneur.com/growing-a-business/5-long-term-strategies-to-build-and-sustain-high-performing/482184

How to Build Systems in Business like an Expert. (2024, April 18). ProcessDriven. https://processdriven.co/workflows/b-workflows/building-business-systems/

Hreha, J. (2023, November 20). *Work-Life Balance: Why It's Important And How To Achieve It.* Persona. https://www.personatalent.com/productivity/how-to-achieve-work-life-balance/

Jenkins, C. (2024, May 3). How to Build High-Performance Leadership Teams for Organizational Success. *Happy Companies.* https://happycompanies.com/blog/building-high-performance-leadership-teams

Ketterer, E. (2023, August 8). Process Standardization: A complete guide. *Celonis.* https://www.celonis.com/blog/process-standardization-a-complete-guide/

Kille, C. (2024, July 4). *What to Do When Personal Values Clash With Business Decisions.* Entrepreneur. https://www.entrepreneur.com/leadership/what-to-do-when-personal-values-clash-with-business/476212

Malets, D. (2023, December 26). *Delegation: Entrust Tasks and Responsibilities to Your Team Members, Develop Their Potential, and Boost Work Efficiency.* Technorely. https://technorely.com/insights/delegation-entrust-tasks-and-responsibilities-to-your-team-members-develop-their-potential-and-boost-work-efficiency

Master Delegation to Boost Productivity and 3X Business Growth. (2024, November 25). *Strategy People Culture Consulting*. https://www.strategypeopleculture.com/blog/delegation-in-leadership/

Mastering Task Delegation: Leveraging Team Strengths and Weaknesses. (2024, September 7). HR Fraternity. https://www.hrfraternity.com/technology-excellence/mastering-task-delegation-leveraging-team-strengths-and-weaknesses.html

Mastrovito, V. (2024, December 20). *From Solo to Scalable: Building Systems to Reduce Owner Dependence*. Prometis Partners. https://www.prometispartners.com/reduce-owner-dependence/

Menon, A. (2023, May 10). *The Four Pillars of Business Scalability for Sustainable Growth*. Medium. https://medium.com/%40menonamrita2/the-four-pillars-of-business-scalability-for-sustainable-growth-de78f49bea63

Nineteen Actions Managers Can Take to Promote Work-Life Balance. (2024, October 15). C-Suite Quarterly. https://csq.com/2024/10/19-actions-managers-can-take-to-promote-work-life-balance/

90-Day Goal Framework: A Structured Approach. (2024, December 16). EF Bomb Coach. https://efbombcoach.com/90-day-goal-framework/

Omrane, A. (2021). Entrepreneurial Burnout: Causes, Consequences and Way Out. *FIIB Business Review*, 7(1), 28–42. https://www.academia.edu/51476249/Entrepreneurial_Burnout_Causes_Consequences_and_Way_Out

Overcoming Delegation Challenges: Strategies for Success. (2024, March 8). HR Fraternity. https://www.hrfraternity.com/leadership-excellence/overcoming-delegation-challenges-strategies-for-success.html

Paras, J. (2024, November 26). *How to use Delegation for building a Strong Team? Learn about Leadership, Personal Development and Project Management*. https://growth-within.com/build-strong-teams-by-using-the-power-of-delegation/#Strategies_for_Building_a_Strong_Team_Through_Delegationnbsp

Penney, S. (2024, July 5). *How to Balance Family and Business - An Entrepreneur's Guide to Harmonious Living*. Entrepreneur. https://www.entrepreneur.com/leadership/how-to-successfully-balance-family-and-business/476372

Quintana, C. (2024, November 27). How To Foster Open Communication In The Workplace. *LineZero*. https://www.linezero.com/blog/how-to-improve-open-communication-in-the-workplace

Ramos, C. (2024, October 20). Transitioning to Team Leadership: A Guide for New Leaders. *Leadership Coach Group*. https://www.leadershipcoachgroup.com/blog/transitioning-to-team-leadership

Sutton, J. (2024, December 12). *12+ Benefits of Goal Setting - Why Goals Are Important*. PositivePsychology.com. https://positivepsychology.com/benefits-goal-setting/

30-60-90 Day Plan: A Guide With Template and Example. (2025). Indeed Career Guide. https://www.indeed.com/career-advice/starting-new-job/30-60-90-day-plan

Tahar, B. Y., Rejeb, N., Maalaoui, A., Kraus, S., Westhead, P., & Jones, P. (2022). *Emotional demands and entrepreneurial burnout: the role of autonomy and job satisfaction*. Small Business Economics, 61(2), 701–716. https://doi.org/10.1007/s11187-022-00702-w

The Art of Delegation – How to Build a Balanced and Scalable Business. (2025). Batemancollective.com. https://www.batemancollective.com/knowledge-hub/the-art-of-delegation---how-to-build-a-balanced-and-scalable-business

The Dangers of Top-Down Leadership and Benefits of Collaborative Leadership. (2024, September 16). Respectful Conversation. https://respectfulconversation.net/the-dangers-of-top-down-leadership-and-benefits-of-collaborative-leadership/

The Role of Delegation in Organizational Growth: A Practical Look. (2024, December 25). Toxigon. https://toxigon.com/the-role-of-delegation-in-organizational-growth

The Role of Visionary Leadership in Business Success. (2024, July 10). Abundance Global. https://www.abundance.global/visionary-leadership-in-business-success/

The Role of Work-Life Balance in Preventing Employee Burnout. (2025). Corporatewellnessmagazine.com. https://www.corporatewellnessmagazine.com/article/the-role-of-work-life-balance-in-preventing-employee-burnout

Thompson, E. (2023, October 13). The Challenges Of Delegating: And How To Overcome Them. *Time Quiver; Ethan Thompson*. https://timequiver.com/blog/time-management-skills/delegation/challenges-delegating-overcome

Unifying Company's Procedures through Process Standardization. (2025, April 2). Cflow. https://www.cflowapps.com/standardized-process/

VanBockel, T. (2024, December 28). *Work-Life Balance Tips for Entrepreneurs in High-Growth Phases*. Attorney Aaron Hall. https://aaronhall.com/work-life-balance-tips-for-entrepreneurs-in-high-growth-phases/

Wesley, C. (2023, October 30). *Visionary Leadership: Unveiling the Secrets to Building a Future-Ready Organization*. Wesley Cherisien. https://wesleycherisien.com/visionary-leadership/

YEC. (2023, June 6). *How To Build A Successful Business And Maintain A Work-Life Balance*. Forbes. https://www.forbes.com/councils/theyec/2023/06/06/how-to-build-a-successful-business-and-maintain-a-work-life-balance/

www.ingramcontent.com/pod-product-compliance
Ingram Content Group UK Ltd.
Pitfield, Milton Keynes, MK11 3LW, UK
UKHW021933190726
13853UKWH00004B/1413